Assessing the Value of Digital Health

Leveraging the HIMSS Value STEPS™ Framework

Assessing the Value of Digital Health

Leveraging the HIMSS Value STEPS™ Framework

By

Kendall Cortelyou-Ward, PhD

Margaret Schulte, DBA, FACHE

Lorren Pettit, MS, MBA

CRC Press
Taylor & Francis Group
Boca Raton London New York

CRC Press is an imprint of the
Taylor & Francis Group, an **informa** business

A PRODUCTIVITY PRESS BOOK

CRC Press
Taylor & Francis Group
6000 Broken Sound Parkway NW, Suite 300
Boca Raton, FL 33487-2742

© 2019 by Taylor & Francis Group, LLC
CRC Press is an imprint of Taylor & Francis Group, an Informa business

No claim to original U.S. Government works

Printed on acid-free paper

International Standard Book Number-13: 978-0-8153-7641-5 (Paperback)
International Standard Book Number-13: 978-1-351-23761-1 (eBook)
International Standard Book Number-13: 978-0-8153-7642-2 (Hardback)

Library of Congress Cataloging-in-Publication Data

Names: Cortelyou-Ward, Kendall, author. | Schulte, Margaret F., author. | Pettit, Lorren, author.
Title: Assessing the value of digital health : leveraging the HIMSS value STEPS framework / Kendall Cortelyou-Ward, Margaret Schulte, Lorren Pettit.
Description: Boca Raton : Taylor & Francis, 2018. | Includes bibliographical references.
Identifiers: LCCN 2018025234 (print) | LCCN 2018026002 (ebook) | ISBN 9781351237611 (e-Book) | ISBN 9780815376415 (pbk. : alk. paper) | ISBN 9780815376422 (hardback : alk. paper)
Subjects: | MESH: Health Care Evaluation Mechanisms--standards | Medical Informatics | Quality of Health Care--standards | United States
Classification: LCC R858 (ebook) | LCC R858 (print) | NLM W 84.4 AA1 | DDC 610.285--dc23
LC record available at https://lccn.loc.gov/2018025234

Visit the Taylor & Francis Web site at
http://www.taylorandfrancis.com

and the CRC Press Web site at
http://www.crcpress.com

Contents

Preface

Healthcare systems the world over have invested significant resources in digital health, also known as health information technology (HIT). The latest forecasts suggest global information technology (IT) spending will rise by 6.2% in 2018, the largest percent increase since 2007, with projected investments to reach $3.74 trillion by the end of the year (Gartner, 2018). Even here in the United States, the federal government through the Center for Medicare and Medicaid Services (CMS) has invested $34.7 billion since 2009 to advance its Meaningful Use (MU) program goals. With so much money devoted to the acquisition of HIT, health leaders have clearly placed a priority on digital health in the delivery of care in today's healthcare system.

Given these large investments, one would assume there would be a well-defined, universally accepted approach for determining the "value" realized from these technologies. Such is not the case. The return on investment in digital health is a complex issue not easy to calculate or immediately clear. The combination of measurable outcomes, such as reduced readmissions, and intangible outcomes, such as staff satisfaction, make determining the value of HIT investments difficult.

This book, entitled *Assessing the Value of Digital Health: Leveraging the HIMSS Value STEPS™ Framework*, explores the Healthcare Information and Management Systems Society (HIMSS) Value STEPS model as a means to assess the various beneficial manifestations of HIT. Once understood, health leaders can use the model to frame conversations around the value HIT provides various stakeholders.

The book divides into eight chapters. Chapter 1 opens by providing a contextual background to the development of the HIMSS Value STEPS™ Framework. More specifically, we explore the shift toward value-based healthcare practice in the United States and the important implications this move has on the growth of digital health. Spurred by legislation to increase health quality, reduce associated costs and place primary focus on the patient, health leaders have leveraged HIT to manage data and data analytics in order to support their delivery of value-based health. In addition, the importance and role of legislation to support developing HIT efforts and programs is discussed.

In Chapters 2 through 7, we turn our attention specifically to the STEPS™ Framework. Comprised of five domains—Satisfaction, Treatment, Electronic Secure Data, Patient Engagement and Population Management and Savings—Chapter 2 provides a high-level overview of the five domains while connecting and exploring each domain's relationship to health information technology. This chapter serves as an introduction to the STEPS™ Framework and each domain.

Chapter 3 addresses the first "S" of the STEPS™ Framework: Satisfaction. Evaluating an array of stakeholders including patients, providers, and staff, our review considers various theories of satisfaction including Maslow's Hierarchy of Needs and the Herzberg Two-Factor Theory to assess the fulfillment of basic, moderate and complex needs.

In Chapter 4, we focus on the "T" of the model: Treatment/Clinical. Here we address the impact of digital health on patient treatment interventions and patient outcomes and the critical relationship between the two. Foundational to our discussion in this chapter is the role clinical measures have in quality of care improvement efforts and how HIT impacts these measures.

Chapter 5 shifts the conversation toward the importance of data security initiatives as we consider the "E" of the STEPS model: Electronic Secure Data. Given the attractiveness of health data to bad actors, provider organizations face ever increasing cybersecurity threats. As the value of a data management system (and ultimately, one's operation) can be severely diminished if the organization's HIT is compromised, health leaders are encouraged to prioritize data security in their daily operations.

The sixth chapter focuses on the benefits of improving and managing populations. Tagged as the "P" of the model, Patient Engagement and Population Management, this chapter explores the value in patient education, engagement and disease prevention in order to affect the organization's bottom line: health outcomes.

We end our review of the STEPS domains in Chapter 7 with the second "S" of the model: Savings. Here we address the importance of documenting the financial implications of HIT for healthcare organizations. Often challenged to reduce costs while simultaneously maintaining a high level of health quality, healthcare providers have been able to leverage HIT to reduce costs and increase profitability by optimizing productivity, advancing efficiency and maximizing return on investment.

We conclude our detailed review of the HIMSS Value STEPS™ Framework in Chapter 8 by detailing the challenges stakeholders may face when applying this model to their own group. Though at first blush the STEPS™ Framework may seem fairly straightforward, there is a complexity to the model that needs to be acknowledged. This chapter offers helpful information and considerations providers should review when determining digital value.

Kendall Cortelyou-Ward, PhD

Reference

Gartner Says Global IT Spending to Grow to 6.2 Percent in 2018. https://www.gartner.com/newsroom/id/3871063. Accessed April 26, 2018.

Acknowledgment

Two individuals were of great help to the authors in lending their expertise and insight to this work. They are Lee Kim and Kathryn Thompson. Their bios follow.

We are immensely appreciative of their work and the value they contributed.

Lee Kim, BS, JD, CISSP, CIPP/US, FHIMSS

Lee Kim is the Director of Privacy and Security at the HIMSS. Kim's roles include subject matter expert, public policy professional and analyst. Kim is a member of the US DHS Analytic Exchange Program. Kim is an AV Preeminent peer review rated attorney in healthcare and intellectual property law.

Kim authors domestic and international works on topics which include information privacy, cybersecurity, law and public policy. Kim's publication credits include GCN, ABA, Digital Health Legal, GCN, Nursing Mgmt. and the California Continuing Education of the Bar.

Kim presents before a variety of audiences—technical, non-technical and legal—for entities which include ABA, CERT/CC, Cisco, ICSJWG, FDA, NIST, OCR/HHS, HC3, Health Care Industry Cybersecurity Taskforce, (ISC)^2, PBI, RSNA, SANS, Sectra AB, Strafford and Verizon.

Kim is a licensed attorney in the District of Columbia and Commonwealth of Pennsylvania and a registered patent attorney with the United States Patent and Trademark Office. Kim is admitted to practice before the District of Columbia Court of Appeals, Supreme Court of Pennsylvania, Western District of Pennsylvania, the Federal Circuit and the United States Patent and Trademark Office. Kim's professional work includes system, network, database, and web administration and application of her legal experience in the fields of intellectual property, information technology, privacy, cybersecurity and healthcare law.

Kathryn Thompson

Kathryn Thompson received her Bachelor of Science (2014) and Master of Health Administration (2017) from the University of Central Florida (UCF). Currently, she is working as a teaching and research assistant at UCF under the guidance of Dr. Kendall Cortelyou-Ward and Dr. Danielle Atkins. Starting Fall 2018, Kathryn will be pursing her PhD in health services research, policy and practice at Brown University in Providence, Rhode Island. She plans to pursue a career in Medicaid policy, focusing on issues related to women and infant health, disparities, vulnerable populations and health outcomes in rural communities.

Authors

Kendall Cortelyou-Ward, PhD is an Associate Professor and Program Director of the Healthcare Informatics Master's Program in the Department of Health Management and Informatics at the University of Central Florida (UCF). She teaches health informatics and information systems courses to graduate and undergraduate students and conducts research in these areas.

Dr. Cortelyou-Ward has over 15 years of professional and academic experience in healthcare management and informatics including serving as the Workforce Director for the UCF Regional Extension Center and as a Research Analyst for the HIMSS Value Suite project. Some previous projects include an evaluation of the use of mobile apps to improve patient outcomes and determination of financial impact of hospitals on the local community. Her current research interests include patient engagement, privacy and security, mixed methods research and the value of health information technology.

Dr. Cortelyou-Ward holds a PhD in public affairs with a specialization in health management research and a master's in health administration from the University of Central Florida. She earned her Bachelor of Science in human resources from the University of Florida.

Margaret F. Schulte, DBA, FACHE (retired) is immediate past President and CEO of the Commission on Accreditation of Healthcare Management Education (CAHME), which is the accrediting body for graduate programs in health administration. Prior to this role, she served on the faculty of the Northwestern University Master of Science in Medical Informatics program, and as editor of *Frontiers in Health Services Management*, a publication of the American College of Healthcare Executives. Previously, she served as Vice President of Education for the Healthcare Information and Management Systems Society (HIMSS), where she was responsible for the domestic and global professional education programs of this membership association of IT professionals.

Dr. Schulte has held positions such as Vice President, Research and Development, for the publishing division of the American Hospital Association (AHA) and Director of Education with the Healthcare Financial Management Association (HFMA), and she served on the faculty of the graduate program in Healthcare Policy and Management at Mercer University in Atlanta, Georgia, where she also served as adjunct faculty to the Mercer University School of Medicine.

Dr. Schulte holds a doctorate in business administration from Nova Southeastern University, Fort Lauderdale, Florida, and a master's in business administration from Xavier University, Cincinnati. She is a Fellow in the American College of Healthcare Executives.

Mr. Lorren Pettit, MS, MBA has been a healthcare researcher and strategist for more than 25 years, with experience in healthcare operations, corporate planning and organizational development. Lorren began his hospital career leading the geriatric behavioral health program for All Saints Health System (Fort Worth, Texas). During his tenure with All Saints, he earned his nursing administrator's license before moving into the health system's strategic planning department. Mr. Pettit transitioned into the hospital alliance/supply chain world with VHA Inc., where he led research/strategic planning activities, before moving into the healthcare patient/provider satisfaction consulting industry with Press Ganey Associates.

He completed his undergraduate work at the University of Winnipeg (Winnipeg, Manitoba, Canada) and achieved a Master of Science in gerontology from Baylor University (Waco, Texas) and a Master of Business Administration from the University of Dallas, Texas. Mr. Pettit served for a number of years as an adjunct faculty member at Indiana University teaching medical sociology, social marketing and gerontology.

Currently, Mr. Pettit is Vice President for HIS and Research for HIMSS. In his current role, he has oversight of four key HIMSS initiatives:

1. HIMSS-sponsored thought leadership research
2. Advancing HIMSS's support of long-term/post-acute care (LTPAC) and behavioral health (BH) information and technology interests
3. Provider use of connected health technologies
4. HIMSS's support of Canadian Digital Health communities

Chapter 1

Background: Why Focus on Digital Health Information Technology Value?

Margaret Schulte

Learning Objectives

- Define healthcare value from the perspective of patient, provider and payer.
- Describe the importance of "value" in the expansion of HIT adoption in the United States
- Frame the evolution and the purpose of public policy in support of HIT.
- Identify and explain incentive programs that spurred the development and implementation of HIT.

Definitions

- *Triple Aim:* A framework developed by the Institute for Healthcare Improvement (IHI) that describes an approach to optimizing health system performance. It is IHI's contention that new designs must be developed to simultaneously pursue three outcomes, which together are called the Triple Aim: (1) Improving the patient experience of care (including quality and satisfaction), (2) improving the health of populations; and (3) reducing the per capita cost of health care (IHI, 2012).

■ *Value-based payment system:* Also known as "performance-based reimbursement." Value-based payment systems provide financial incentives to healthcare providers for meeting performance improvement measures. Those measures are designed to achieve improved quality of care.

Introduction

U.S. healthcare delivery organizations today face a new challenge as well as a new opportunity: to improve the patient experience of care and the health of populations while reducing the per capita cost of healthcare. This chapter focuses on how the provider market's demand for data and information to achieve new measures of value has accelerated the adoption of electronic health records (EHR) and other digital technologies (e.g. mobile, telehealth). Driven by multiple forces including the Triple Aim, changing reimbursement structures and the Agency for Healthcare Research and Quality (AHRQ), the federal government's leading agency charged with improving the quality, safety, efficiency and effectiveness of health care for all Americans, efforts to realize these concurrent goals have pushed U.S. healthcare organizations to re-focus healthcare delivery on "value" rather than "volume."

In the transition from volume to value, provider success is based on the assumption of risk and the expectation that the delivery system can accurately assess its performance and the health of its population. Value-based payment methods have been designed to incentivize the achievement of improvements in quality and to drive cost reduction. Core to the development of value-based payment design is the availability of information systems and the analytics that support users in clinical and management decisions. Indeed, delivering value as prescribed by the Triple Aim is too complex without the aid of supportive technologies. The AHRQ defines quality health care "as doing the right thing for the right patient, at the right time, in the right way to achieve the best possible results" (AHRQ, 2003).

The digital record for example, supports the identification and adoption of measurable quality goals. Performance can therefore be evaluated against the goals on each of these measures. Consequently, access to data and the insight its analysis provides are critical to the success of transitioning to value-based care.

In this chapter, we focus on the factors driving U.S. healthcare providers to embrace this new definition of value in healthcare, as well as the concurrent demand for data and information to achieve new measures of value. We also spend some time exploring the forces driving the ubiquitous adoption of EHRs and other digital technologies in order to gain improved outcomes in the health of the population. Financial incentives and delivery structures, supported by information technology, have been put in place to derive value in improved quality of care and efficiency that otherwise would not be possible. Case #1.1, Nicklaus Children's Hospital, provides an example of improved quality that was made possible because of the availability of an EHR. Discussion of these incentives and structures and their relationship to performance improvement for increased value follows.

> ## CASE #1.1: THE NICKLAUS CHILDREN'S HOSPITAL— REDUCING BLOOD TRANSFUSION ERROR
>
> Errors in blood transfusion practices can lead to serious consequences. The majority of errors occur due to the incorrect sampling of blood from a patient, obtaining the wrong unit of blood for a patient, or transfusing blood inappropriately. The Nicklaus Children's Hospital was able to drop blood transfusion error rates to zero using barcoding technology.
>
> *Source:* HIMSS, 2017b: Miami Children's Health System.

Background

Michael Porter, the renowned American economist, says that:

> [A]chieving high value for patients must become the overarching goal of health care delivery, with value defined as the health outcomes achieved per dollar spent. This goal is what matters for patients and unites the interests of all actors in the system. If value improves, then patients, payers, providers, and suppliers can all benefit while the economic sustainability of the health care system increases.
>
> **Porter, 2010**

In the complex world of healthcare, value is too often defined subjectively based on individual roles or perspectives, i.e. those of the patient, provider, payer, regulator, etc. In a system that is already very complex, these perspectives can be in conflict. The individual or group perception of value may focus on one or a number of values such as access, satisfaction, efficiency, profitability, quality of care, cost savings, personal work ethic, etc.

Even with the best of intentions, achieving the highest health outcomes per dollar spent (i.e. high-level quality and improved efficiency) has been too often thwarted due to lack of data to support goals of measurable improved outcomes. For decades, healthcare providers cast "value" as something other than specific patient outcomes. Rather, it was expressed in vague statements such as "we provide high-quality care" and "the patient is our first concern." These "truisms" were accepted when analytical data was not available to confirm or demonstrate otherwise. Even though we are in the infancy of healthcare information technology implementation and data analytics, the data that has already been generated is being used by organizations to achieve measurable performance improvement. For example, Case #1.2; describes how Parkland Health and Hospital System achieved a reduction in sepsis because they had the tools to identify early indications of possible sepsis. Given the organization's access to the detailed data that digital technology provided on each patient, clinicians at Parkland were able to improve compliance with significant quality improvement measures from 14% to 29%.

CASE #1.2: PARKLAND HEALTH AND HOSPITAL SYSTEM

Parkland Health and Hospital System used innovative mobile solutions for sepsis alerts by aggregating multiple patient-specific measures in real-time to estimate the risk of a patient being classified as septic. Parkland's sepsis bundle compliance improved from 14% to 29%. The average and median length-of-stay reductions for Sepsis POA (present-on-admission) patients were 21.5% and 12.6%, respectively.

Source: HIMSS, 2017c: Parkland Health and Hospital System.

With the publication of the 1999 Institute of Medicine (IOM) report "To err is human: Building a safer health system," healthcare leaders came face-to-face with credible data related to the numbers of preventable patient deaths and injuries that were happening within the care delivery system—almost 100,000 deaths each year. Preventable errors occur due in large part to unintentional human error and lack of information to recognize, measure and correct. As Don Berwick, MD, President Emeritus and Senior Fellow,

IHI, put it: "We must accept human error as inevitable—and design around that fact" (IHI, 2018).

Prior to the publication of the IOM report, healthcare providers were at a major disadvantage to gauge their performance in that they did not have the information to see themselves in the "data mirror." Once they saw and accepted the data, they recognized that they had to take steps to change performance outcomes. They had to determine where to focus, to design and to implement the necessary clinical measures and processes for change. More detailed data was needed, and it was only going to be accessed through information technology. According to HIMSS:

> IT provides organizations with the means to assess their value-based care optimization efforts, create their HIT optimization strategies, achieve their goals, gain recognition for their efforts, and finally, share their success stories with others like them—all by leveraging the power of people, processes and technology to transform health and healthcare through IT.
>
> **HIMSS, 2016**

Finding Value in HIT: A Brief History

For decades, going back to the 1960s and 1970s, there was a small but growing number of professionals in healthcare actively viewing the EHR as an essential tool to collect meaningful data and, with it, improve healthcare delivery and outcomes. This was an elite group of very early adopters of what were rudimentary information systems when the EHR was introduced. However, it was only after decades of gradual progress in developing the technology, of dramatically rising healthcare costs, and the publication of the 1999 IOM report that the number of voices advocating for the EHR became strong enough to effectively press for a national initiative to significantly boost the path to the adoption of EHRs throughout the healthcare system. Policy makers, payers and providers generally agreed that something had to be done to address rising costs and to stop the many fatal and/or harmful, but preventable, outcomes that occur in varied healthcare settings. In its report, the IOM directly addressed the need for IT in healthcare. They concluded, among other things, that healthcare would be safer with such systems as computerized physician order entry (CPOE) in place to reduce medical errors that result from causes such as indecipherable handwriting. More and better information was believed to be the answer that would drive better decision-making, more efficient processes, and better outcomes (i.e. better value).

Within 5 years of the release of the IOM report, President George W. Bush allocated $50 million in the FY 2004 federal budget to provide grants to local and regional organizations to develop systems for information sharing. A year later, in the FY 2005 budget, he took this a substantial step further when he increased the funding to $100 million calling for "widespread adoption of electronic health records in 10 years," (Healthcare IT News, 2004) and created, by Executive Order, the sub-Cabinet Office of National Health Information Coordinator. The $100 million funding was designated for EHR demonstration projects throughout the country to pave the way for widespread adoption.

According to White House documentation on this initiative, the President believed "that innovations in EHR and the secure exchange of medical information will help transform healthcare in America" (Healthcare IT News, 2004). In the end, this meant reducing preventable deaths and improving clinical outcomes, advancing the health of the population and gaining efficiencies.

The march toward the ubiquitous implementation of EHRs in U.S. healthcare organizations was propelled with the signing of the American Recovery and Reinvestment Act of 2009 (ARRA) by President Barack Obama in February 2009. One section of the Act, the Health Information Technology for Economic and Clinical Health Act (HITECH), provided for incentive payments to healthcare providers who met "Meaningful Use" criteria. These criteria called for using an EHR for relevant purposes and meeting specified technological requirements. Passed by Congress, the Act gave new life and funding to ONC and the nationwide incentive to implement EHRs. The Meaningful Use program was created and funded to reward hospitals, doctors and other providers for their EHR implementation and achievement of measurable quality focused criteria. Initial criteria focused on basic levels of adoption and indicators of quality improvement. As the program's three stages progressed, increasingly sophisticated quality measures were implemented to reflect greater depth of Meaningful Use of the EHR and greater value in healthcare delivery.

By 2015, nearly 9 in 10 (87%) office-based physicians had adopted some type of an EHR, with over 3 in 4 (78%) having adopted an EHR certified by the federal government, satisfying specific criteria. As of 2016, over 95% of all eligible and Critical Access Hospitals (CAH) had demonstrated Meaningful Use of certified HIT (ONC, 2017).

DEFINITION: CAH

CAH designation is provided to certain hospitals in order to *reduce the financial vulnerability* of rural hospitals and *improve access to healthcare* by keeping essential services in rural communities. To qualify for CAH designation, hospitals must:

- Have 25 or fewer acute care inpatient beds.
- Generally, be located more than 35 miles from another hospital.
- Maintain an annual average length-of-stay of 96 hours or less for acute care patient.
- Provide 24/7 emergency care services.

Source: RHIhub, 2017.

Widespread adoption of EHRs occurred at an accelerated pace due in part to the financial incentives of the Meaningful Use program and of performance-based reimbursement systems. Clinicians also came to see that in order to achieve dramatic improvement in clinical care, they finally had the critical tools to make it happen. Clinicians had been confronted with the stark reality of the data revealed in the IOM report, and with the data collected and analyzed by electronic systems, it was now possible to pinpoint opportunities to reduce errors and improve outcomes.

A CMIO'S PERSPECTIVE ON THE IMPORTANCE OF THE EHR

Data will be at the center of knowledge discovery and decision support. We previously have had to rely on traditional medical studies with knowledge discovery cycles taking years. Even when the process yielded valid insights, it was often difficult to validate these external insights to one's own organization. New data infrastructures speed this process and allow organizations to use their own data to discover associations and knowledge precisely focused on their particular patient population and workflows. We will essentially be able to industrialize complex, precise knowledge discovery.

John Lee, 2017

Value-Based Incentive Payment Models

The investment in HIT represented a significant commitment by the country and healthcare providers to improve clinical, financial and patient-focused quality outcomes. To achieve that improvement, both administrative management and clinical professionals needed analytics to pull meaningful information from the data in order to improve complex clinical and organizational decisions. The data was critical to improvement of their individual and organizational performance.

Data and analytics allowed new payment structures to evolve to replace the long-standing fee-for-service model and to further incentivize performance improvement. The new value-based payment structures are designed to ensure that healthcare providers would be paid for the value they contribute to clinical outcomes and population health, not for the volume of care they delivered. The incentives took providers through a 180-degree turn from a focus on volume toward a focus on clinical outcomes, i.e. on quality improvement.

While there are a number of value-based payment structures in both the private and public payer programs, three of the more common programs will be discussed briefly below: (1) the patient-centered medical home (PCMH), (2) the physician quality reporting system (PQRS) and its successor merit-based incentive payment system (MIPS), and (3) accountable care organizations (ACOs).

Patient-Centered Delivery of Care: The Patient-Centered Medical Home

The PCMH is defined by the Patient-Centered Primary Care Collaborative (PCPCC) as "a model or philosophy of primary care that is patient-centered, comprehensive, team-based, coordinated, accessible, and focused on quality and safety. It has become a widely accepted model for how primary care should be organized and delivered throughout the health care system" (Defining the Medical Home, 2017). In the PCMH, patients are treated as a population, and "HIT is essential for optimal management of that population's care" (Basch et al., 2015).

The PCMH model was designed as an approach to primary care delivery to achieve improved outcomes as it addresses the high incidence and cost of chronic disease in defined U.S. populations. Overall, the U.S. incidence of persons with one or more chronic conditions continues to be high. According to the Centers for Disease Control and Prevention (CDC) as of 2012, "about half of all adults—117 million people—had one or more chronic health conditions" (CDC, 2016). The population with one or more chronic conditions places a major burden on the cost of medical care in the country. As the CDC reports further, "Eighty-six percent of the nation's $2.7 trillion annual health care expenditures are for people with chronic and mental health conditions" (CDC, 2016). This speaks only of direct healthcare costs, it does not address the economic cost of lost productivity of patients who are unable to work and of non-paid caregivers. The value equation for healthcare would suggest that success in achieving improved outcomes for patients with chronic disease can reduce the overall burden of healthcare costs on the economy.

The opportunity for value creation in population health alone is high. The PCMH design addresses this, and HIT is essential to data analysis and reporting by informing processes that ultimately lead to outcomes improvement for patients, providers and payers. In fact, a PCMH cannot qualify for its designation with the National Committee for Quality Assurance (NCQA) unless it has HIT available. The white paper issued by the AHRQ details the need for HIT in the PCMH:

> Adoption of the PCMH model calls for fundamental changes in the way many primary care practices operate, including adoption of health information technology (IT) both for internal processes and for connecting the practice with its patients and with other providers. Health IT has been promoted as a "disruptive innovation" that offers tremendous promise for transforming health care delivery systems, including primary care.

Moreno, Peikes and Krilla, 2010

Physician Quality Reporting System (PQRS)

The PQRS encourages individual eligible professionals (EPs) and group practices to report to Medicare on the quality of care they provide to their patients. PQRS gives participating EPs and group practices the opportunity to assess the quality of care they provide to their patients, helping to ensure that patients get the right care at the right time. In order to provide reports of progress in quality of care, physicians must have the information systems that can provide the relevant data.

Under the new value-based payment structure:

> Physicians need more data and analytics to succeed. For physicians
> seeing hundreds of patients, navigating requirements that vary by
> benefit type, health plan, and patient, treatment is nearly impos-
> sible. Technology has the potential to alleviate this complexity,
> empowering physicians to identify and close gaps in quality, risk,
> and utilization—essentially in real-time and within their current
> workflow processes.

L. P. James, 2017

In further pursuit of improved quality, the PQRS program began in
2015 to apply a *negative* payment adjustment to individual EPs and PQRS
group practices satisfactorily reporting data on quality measures under the
Medicare Part B Physician Fee Schedule (PFS) professional services for the
year 2013. In short, EPs would experience a punitive financial result if they
did not report.

As of 2017, PQRS evolved with the implementation of the MIPS. Under
MIPS, providers are not only required to have certified information systems
but are prohibited from blocking or limiting the interoperability of their EHR
with other systems. They are required to ensure that data can be shared
from their system to other providers and payers. Under this program, physicians earn an upward payment adjustment formulated on their submission of data documenting achievement of practice specific goals that are
evidence-based.

Accountable Care Organizations (ACOs)

ACOs are groups of hospitals, doctors, ambulatory care organizations and
other health care providers who voluntarily organize with each other to give
coordinated high-quality care to the patient populations that they serve, particularly the chronically ill. They strive to ensure that their patients get the
right care at the right time, while avoiding duplication of services. When an
ACO succeeds in delivering high-quality care and managing costs, it shares
in the savings it achieves. As reported by Schultz, DeCamp and Berkowitz
in June 2017, there were 434 ACOs participating in Medicare and serving
over 7 million beneficiaries. As ACOs continue to advance in size and number, it is important for both providers and payers to ensure that risk is being

appropriately shared between the two entities. This creates a unique set of challenges in determining the best way to design, manage and evaluate these programs.

According to HIMSS, the transformation of health providers into ACOs has dramatic implications for the cost/access/quality equation in healthcare, and profound strategic and structural ramifications for providers (HIMSS, 2017a). Among these ramifications is the assumption of financial risk by ACOs in care delivery. This demands information and supportive systems to receive, store and analyze information, as well as utilize risk algorithms to quantitatively assess the morbidity risks of the patient populations served.

According to a report published by Truven Health Analytics (a healthcare data and analytics company), early results suggest that ACOs are transforming patient care. Collectively, in the first two performance years, ACOs in the MSSP realized a total net savings of $848 million for the Medicare Trust Funds. They have also shown improvement in 27 out of 33 quality measures, leading to $656 million in shared savings payments (Azzolini, 2016).

Summary

Value in healthcare has been defined succinctly by some as health outcomes achieved by dollar spent (Porter, 2010). While other experts may add concepts to the definition of value in healthcare, each gets back to the same fundamental elements: outcomes and costs. It is the next level of definition of each of these two factors that has long been difficult to pin down. Outcomes and costs may vary depending on the perspective of the stakeholder, e.g. those of the provider may differ from those of the patient, and cost perspectives may differ between those of the finance expert and those of the patient whose life and health are impacted. Measurement of outcomes is essential to their accomplishment, and measurement requires specific data. Getting that data requires, in turn, technology. Here is where the essential value of the EHR can be found. It provides the data to recognize, understand and assess outcomes and the performance requirements for improvement.

Discussion Questions

1. How do you define value in healthcare? What are the strengths and weaknesses of your definition?

2. What were the Stage 1, 2 and 3 reporting requirements under the Meaningful Use program and when was each implemented? What were the most significant HIT developments and impediments to implementation of each stage? How did these, or did they not, serve to improve performance outcomes in healthcare? Was the Meaningful Use program of value to healthcare in the United States? Explain your answer.

3. What are performance payment systems? How do they work? Identify two or three models of performance payment (try to find one or more that are not described in this chapter). How effective are these systems in creating measurable value? Discuss their pro's and con's.

CASE FOR DISCUSSION: THE CLEVELAND CLINIC

Cleveland Clinic, a nonprofit multispecialty academic medical center and 2017 HIMSS Enterprise Davies Award Recipient, leverages information and technology to more effectively identify at-risk patients and predict the need for care interventions to reduce patient mortality and unnecessary readmissions. Over 1,500 patients were being monitored and processed through the organization's heart failure checklist. Electronic Checklist compliance was much higher versus paper. Cleveland Clinic had an enterprise target of reducing their readmission rate to 20% compared to the typical range of 25%. With the electronic checklist, they were able to meet that target.

After the implementation of the VitalScout program, the pilot hospital was able to decrease by more than a third, the number of cardiac arrests in their medical/surgical unit. By 2017, the hospital had gone on to demonstrate a 50% decrease in codes from pre-implementation numbers.

Prior to the hypertension improvement intervention, Cleveland Clinic was only able to garner 87% of the ACO quality points. After the intervention, they achieved 96% of the ACO quality points. The quality improvement in 2016 translated to an additional $3 million dollars.

Source: HIMSS, 2017d: Cleveland Clinic: Davies Enterprise Award.

DISCUSSION QUESTIONS

The Cleveland Clinic has achieved multiple value benefits from the use of its digital technology. List all the values that you can identify in this case. How does each serve to advance performance improvement for the Clinic, for patients, for payers and for the community? What challenges might they have faced in achieving these values? How would you address those challenges? What do you think are other areas of value that may have been achieved?

References

AHRQ. A quick look at quality. 2003. https://archive.ahrq.gov/consumer/qnt/qntq-look.htm. Accessed October 15, 2017.

Azzolini J. The Five Key Components of ACO Analytics. http://truvenhealth.com/blog/the-five-key-components-of-aco-analytics. August 30, 2016. Accessed October 20, 2017.

Basch P, McClellan M, Botts C, Katikaneni P. High value health IT: Policy reforms for better care and lower costs. March 2015. The Brookings Institution Health Policy Issue Brief.

CDC (Centers for Disease Control and Prevention). Chronic disease prevention and health promotion. Chronic disease overview. January 11, 2016. www.cdc.gov/chronicdisease/overview/index.htm. Accessed October 17, 2017.

Defining the Medical Home. Patient-centered primary care collaborative. 2017. www.pcpcc.org/about/medical-home Accessed October 24, 2017.

Healthcare IT News. President Bush continues push, sets national goals. April 26, 2004. https://www.healthcareitnews.com/news/president-bush-continues-ehr-push-sets-national-goals. Accessed July 18, 2018.

HIMSS. What is the value suite? homepage. 2016. www.himss.org/valuesuite. Accessed October 11, 2017.

HIMSS. Accountable care home page. 2017a. www.himss.org/library/accountable-care. Accessed November 11, 2017.

HIMSS. Miami Children's Health System: Davies Enterprise Award. 2017b. www.himss.org/library/nicklaus-children-s-hospital-davies-enterprise-award. Accessed October 20, 2017.

HIMSS. Parkland Health and Hospital System. 2017c. www.himss.org/library/parkland-health-hospital-system-davies-enterprise-award. Accessed April 29, 2018.

HIMSS. Cleveland Clinic: Davies Enterprise Award. 2017d. https://www.himss.org/library/cleveland-clinic-davies-enterprise-award. Accessed August 3, 2018.

IHI (Institute for Healthcare Improvement). Initiatives: IHI triple aim initiative. 2012. www.ihi.org/engage/initiatives/TripleAim/Pages/default.aspx. Accessed October 15, 2017.

IHI (Institute for Healthcare Improvement). Improvement stories: Want a new level of performance? Get a new system. 2018. http://www.ihi.org/resources/Pages/ImprovementStories/WantaNewLevelofPerformanceGetaNewSystem.aspx. Accessed October 24, 2017.

James, LP. Extending the value of the EHR. *Health Management Technology.* August 29, 2017. https://www.healthmgttech.com/extending-value-ehr. Accessed October 24, 2017.

Lee J. A CMIOs perspective on Health 2.0. October 18, 2017. www.himss.org/news/cmios-perspective-health-20. Accessed October 23, 2017.

Moreno L, Peikes D and Krilla A. Mathmetica policy research. Necessary but not sufficient: The HITECH Act and healthcare information technology's potential to build medical homes. AHRQ. Publication No. 10-0080-EF. June 2010. https://pcmh.ahrq.gov/sites/default/files/attachments/necessary-but-not-sufficient-hitech-act-white-paper.pdf. Accessed October 20, 2017.

ONC (Office of the National Healthcare Coordinator). Health IT dashboard: Quick stats. https://dashboard.healthit.gov/quickstats/quickstats.php. Posted August 3, 2017. Accessed October 20, 2017.

Porter ME. What is value in health care? 2010. *N Engl J Med* 363:2477–2481.

RHIhub. Critical access hospitals. 2017. www.ruralhealthinfo.org/topics/critical-access-hospitals. Accessed October 24, 2018.

Chapter 2

HIMSS Value STEPS™ Framework

Margaret Schulte

Learning Objectives

- Define the five categories of the HIMSS Value STEPS™ Framework and their relationship to digital technologies in healthcare.
- Articulate the inter-relationships between the five categories in the HIMSS Value STEPS™ Framework.
- Apply the STEPS™ 5-domain Framework to assess the value(s) derived from an EHR and other healthcare digital technologies.

Definitions

- *CAUTI*: Catheter-associated urinary tract infection.
- *EMRAM (electronic medical records adoption model)*: A tool developed by HIMSS Analytics guiding hospitals to improved clinical outcomes.
- *Davies Award*: The HIMSS Nicholas E. Davies Award of Excellence recognizes outstanding achievement of organizations who have utilized health information technology to substantially improve patient outcomes and value.

Introduction

The STEPS™ Framework was developed in response to the challenges the Meaningful Use (MU) program posed for U.S. hospitals and providers. Under MU, billions of taxpayer dollars were committed to the adoption of EHRs throughout the U.S. healthcare delivery system. The program was designed to provide incentive payments to eligible hospitals and providers to implement EHRs. These incentives helped to offset the significant investment required to acquire and implement information technology. The transition from paper to information technology was formidable for many hospitals and providers. Many began to question the level and kinds of value they would get for the investments they and taxpayers were making in the conversion to information technology. The market (hospitals and healthcare systems as well as non-institutional providers of care such as ambulatory care centers, physicians, public health agencies, long-term care providers, community health centers and others impacted by the MU program), clearly needed an approach for delineating and documenting the quantifiable and qualitative benefits healthcare organizations and individuals utilizing the digital health record could achieve.

The HIMSS Value STEPS™ Framework was designed to be a useful tool to help inform organizations and individuals in meeting a variety of needs. It provides an easily understood vocabulary for stakeholders to leverage when formulating strategies related to operating in a value-based business model. The STEPS™ Framework is built around five major categories of value that can be driven through the use of HIT. The five major domains as described by HIMSS in The HIT Value STEPS™ Framework are:

1. Satisfaction

   This domain focuses on people, process and technology that demonstrate increased stakeholders' satisfaction with the delivery of care. Satisfaction includes the sub-domains:
   – Patient satisfaction
   – Provider satisfaction
   – Staff satisfaction

2. Treatment/Clinical

   Value in the treatment and/or clinical area focuses on effective and improved treatment of patients, reduction in medical errors and inappropriate/duplicate care, and increases in safety, quality of care and

overall clinical efficiencies. The Treatment/Clinical value domain includes the sub-domains:
– Efficiencies
– Quality of care
– Safety

3. Electronic Secure Information/Data
   This domain focuses on improved data capture, data sharing, reporting, use of evidence-based medicine, and improved communication by and between physicians, staff and patients. Electronic Secure Data includes the sub-domains:
   – Privacy and security
   – Data sharing
   – Data reporting
   – Enhanced communication

4. Patient Engagement and Population Management
   This domain focuses on improved population health and reduction in disease due to improved surveillance/screening, immunizations and increased patient engagement due to improved patient education and access to information. The Patient Engagement and Population Management domain includes sub-domains:
   – Patient education
   – Patient engagement
   – Prevention
   – Screenings

5. Savings
   In this domain, the Savings value focuses on documented financial, operational and efficiency resulting from factors such as improved charge capture, improved use of staff resources and workflow and improved scheduling of patients. In addition to efficiency, Savings sub-domains include financial/business savings such as increased patient revenue and reduction in days in accounts receivable. The sub-domain of operational savings addresses factors such as improved use of space and disaster preparedness (HIMSS, 2018a).

Each of the value domains and sub-domains are exemplified by specific identifiable, often measurable, examples. These examples can be found in further detail in Appendix 3: "HIMSS Value STEPS™ Framework Domains and Examples."

While each of the five major domains of value are defined separately, in many cases, they also have a relationship with one another. In their relational mode, often one value domain is more dominant than any one or more of the other four domains. A Children's National Health System scenario (Case #2.1) exemplifies this issue. In this case, the value that is dominant is in the domain of Treatment/Clinical. Utilization of clinical best practices is advanced when information is offered in digital format in the EHR. Quality of care is improved with the resultant reduction in children's exposure to CAUTI. Additionally, medication reconciliation is improved by reducing medication errors, and patient safety is advanced in the reduced exposure to unnecessary radiation. Value within the domain of Electronic Secure Information/Data emerges in the improved accuracy of patient records, and value within the Savings domain is suggested in the phrase "generate significant return on investment."

In other words, while the STEPS™ Framework brings different value domains into focus, the analyst may assess the value in any one category, but may also find it useful to consider or acknowledge the relatedness of other values, albeit of less or equal emphasis.

CASE #2.1: CHILDREN'S NATIONAL HEALTH SYSTEM

Children's National Health System, a 2017 HIMSS Enterprise Nicholas E. Davies Award of Excellence recipient, stands at the forefront of using electronic quality boards to enable enhanced adherence to utilizing clinical best practice for reducing children's exposure to CAUTI while improving medication reconciliation and reducing exposure to unnecessary radiation. IT-enabled clinical documentation improvements improve accuracy of patient records and generate significant return on investment.

Source: HIMSS, 2017: Children's National Health System: Davies Enterprise Award.

When utilizing the HIMSS Value STEPS™ for analysis or reporting from the literature, there are two principles that should be kept in mind:

1. *Recognition of the origin of qualitative data.* In gathering qualitative data, it is important to understand the individual perspective of the survey respondent or source of information. A nurse, for instance, will have a different perspective from that of someone in finance. While both may have the same data, it will likely mean something different to

each. For example, when an article or report from the literature is referenced, the audience for which that article or report was written will be reflected in the focus of the literature. Again, if it is written for a nursing audience, then the focus will likely be more clinical than an article written for an audience of financial professionals.

2. *The priority of human behavior.* As noted in an earlier chapter, while the intent of the HIMSS Value STEPS™ Framework is to assess the value of digital information technologies from five key organizational domains or interest areas, the human factor is essential to the value that is achieved in using digital technology. Value will be achieved only to the extent that human users actually use the technology correctly and consistently. Consequently, analysis should consider the human factor as a key context for the data.

Summary

The HIMSS Value STEPS™ Framework has been widely adopted as a resource to guide assessment of the value of digital health technologies such as the EHR, mobile health, telehealth and other related technologies. The STEPS™ Framework is designed around five domains of value that are important to healthcare organizations and providers of care:

- **S**atisfaction
- **T**reatment/Clinical care
- **E**lectronic Secure Data and information
- **P**atient Engagement And Population Management
- **S**avings

The STEPS™ Framework offers a useful way to identify the benefit derived from information technologies and to help organizations and individuals to assess, problem solve, measure and achieve performance improvement.

Discussion Questions

1. When the HIMSS Value STEPS™ Framework was designed, it fulfilled a need that hospitals and healthcare systems and other providers of care needed to justify the significant financial and organizational investment

they were making in information technology. Today, that investment has been made and EHRs are in almost every provider organization in the country. What do you think drives the need for HIT value realization assessment today?

2. How is the achievement of the IHI's Triple Aim furthered through the use of healthcare IT?

3. Is the EHR worth the investment of time and funding that has been spent on it in the last decade?

Case Exercises

In each of the following real life scenarios, identify the relevant STEPS™ Value Framework categories. Would you assess the values as having equal emphasis or is one more dominant than the other(s) based on the way in which the scenario is written? Explain.

EXERCISE CASE #2.1: HORIZON FAMILY MEDICAL GROUP

To improve patient engagement with the intention of enhancing patient care and outcomes, the 2016 Davies Ambulatory Awardee, Horizon Family Medical Group (HFMG) adopted a new focus from reactive to preventative medicine. New workflows lead to improvements in provider and patient interaction.

HFMG increased patient engagement, face-to-face time by 27% for 15-minute appointment time slots with the help of the built-in workflow tools such as the Huddle Report. Counseling face-to-face time increased by 20% for a 20-minutes appointment time slots. The Huddle Report helped increase compliancy for PQRS and HEDIS programs that led to increased financial reimbursements in incentive dollars (HIMSS, 2016).

EXERCISE CASE #2.2: ADVOCATE HEALTH: MONITORING BLOOD PRODUCT ORDERS

In 2011, Advocate Health identified a high level of variability among patients who received blood products. Clinical leaders were challenged to develop guidelines to direct blood product use with real-time EHR decision support. Clinical users were presented with the system guidelines and the patient's specific test results before blood products could be ordered. No user was stopped from ordering blood, but they had to enter a reason why they were ordering blood outside the guidelines. The blood product leadership team circulated utilization reports generated by the EHR team each quarter to help identify outliers and encourage behavior change. The initiative reduced blood product utilization by nearly 50% over the first year with sustained reductions five years later.

Advocate Health saved about 9.1 million dollars by reducing overuse of blood products. They went from actual spending of $26.5 million in 2011 to $17.4 million in 2016. For Advocate Health's Level 1 trauma center, there was a 47% decrease of red blood cell (RBC) utilization and a 59% decrease in RBC utilization for non-level I trauma center. Advocate's clinical leaders attribute the project's success to a combination of effective project management, targeted EHR decision support and reporting to monitor and impact guideline adherence (HIMSS, 2018b).

EXERCISE CASE #2.3: MEMORIAL HERMANN: HIT IMPROVING PATIENT CARE

Memorial Hermann is using data to prevent ventilator-acquired pneumonia (VAP) in patients. Studies have found that up to 20% of ventilated patients in hospitals across the United States develop VAP, and at least 20% of those cases may be preventable.

Memorial Hermann also created documentation bundles aimed at driving best practices to prevent central line associated blood stream infections (CLABSIs). As many as 28,000 people die every year from CLABSIs in ICU units across the United States, according to the U.S. Department of Health and Human Services. To tackle this problem, Memorial Hermann tailored IT interventions to fit into different clinical workflows and the team provides consistent monitoring on an ongoing basis to ensure success.

"Memorial Hermann's 'good catches' for clinical decision support, VAP bundle and focus on CLABSIs demonstrates how clinical decision support enables significant improvements in patient safety" (HIMSS, 2018c).

References

HIMSS. Horizon Family Medical Group. 2016. www.himss.org/library/horizon-family-medical-group. Accessed March 7, 2018.

HIMSS. Children's National Health System: Davies Enterprise Award. 2017. www. himss.org/library/children-s-national-healthsystem-davies-enterprise-award.

HIMSS. The HIMSS Health Value STEPS™. 2018a. www.himss.org/valuesuite/ valuesteps#step-28346. Accessed March 1, 2018.

HIMSS. Advocate Health Care: Leveraging health IT to achieve patient, physician and cost benefits. 2018b. www.himss.org/news/leveraging-health-it-achieve-patient-physician-and-cost-benefits. Accessed March 7, 2018.

HIMSS. Memorial Hermann: Data-driven process improvement. 2018c. www.himss. org/news/utilizing-health-data-provide-safer-patient-care. Accessed March 7, 2018.

Chapter 3

Satisfaction

Kendall Cortelyou-Ward

Learning Objectives

- Evaluate Maslow's Hierarchy of Needs and how it relates to patients, healthcare providers and staff.
- Evaluate the Herzberg Two-Factor Theory and how it relates to patients, healthcare providers and staff.
- Analyze the impact HIT has on provider, staff and patient satisfaction.

Definitions

- *Satisfaction*: The pleasure derived from an individual's fulfillment of wishes, expectations or needs.
- *CPOE (Computerized Practitioner Order Entry)*: An order entry application specifically designed to assist practitioners in creating and managing medical orders for patient services and medications. This application has special electronic signature, workflow and rules engine functions that reduce or eliminate medical errors associated with practitioner ordering processes.
- *PACS (picture archiving and communication systems)*: A system that begins by converting the standard storage of x-ray files into digitized electronic media that can later be retrieved by radiologists, clinicians and other staff to view exam data and medical images.

■ *E-prescribing*: The use of computing devices to enter, modify, review and output or communicate drug prescriptions.

■ *Motivating factors*: Those characteristics of a job that arise from intrinsic satisfaction.

■ *Hygiene factors*: Those characteristics of a job that are external to the actual work.

■ *Deprivation needs*: Lack of satisfaction causes a deficiency that motivates people to meet these needs.

Introduction

Satisfaction is a highly studied construct that in its most basic form is the pleasure derived from an individual's fulfillment of wishes, expectations or needs. In any healthcare organization, one has to balance the satisfaction of numerous stakeholders that influence clinical and financial outcomes. Given the unique nature of the healthcare setting, this balance requires knowledge of motivators, satisfiers and dissatisfiers for each stakeholder group. There are numerous theories that can guide interventions to maximize both employee and patient satisfaction

Theories of Satisfaction

Maslow's Hierarchy of Needs

One of the most famous theoretical frameworks surrounding the fulfillment of needs and satisfaction is Maslow's Hierarchy of Needs. James Maslow introduced this foundational theory in 1943 in his paper titled "A theory of human motivation" in which he presented the idea that humans will direct their behavior toward the attainment of a goal and that certain needs must be satisfied before higher order needs can be fulfilled. For example, if an individual is without a home, their primary motivation is to find a place to live, not to form friendships as represented in the higher "belonging" level. The theory is most commonly represented as a triangle (please see Figure 3.1: Maslow's Hierarchy of Needs) with basic or physiological needs forming the base and moving up to self-actualization where an individual realizes their full potential.

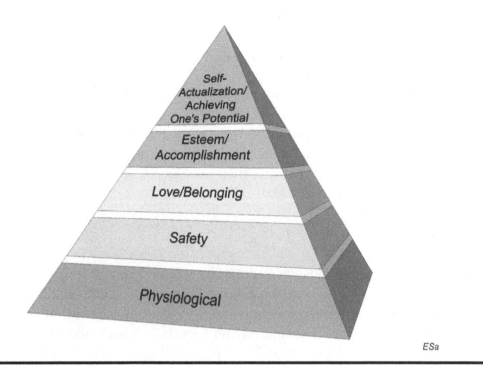

ESa

Figure 3.1   Maslow's Hierarchy of Needs.

Deprivation Needs

The bottom four categories of Maslow's Hierarchy, also known as the deprivation needs, include those needs that if not met, create such a deprivation in one's life that they must be satisfied for progression to self-actualization. With the exception of physiological needs, a deficit in these deprivation needs often has no physical manifestation; rather, an individual may simply feel anxious and tense and therefore unable to achieve satisfaction.

Basic Needs

Of the deprivation needs, the physiological needs are the most basic for human survival including food, shelter and clothing. Given the fundamental nature of physiological needs all energy will be used to meet those needs before safety, belonging, and esteem can be addressed. In the workplace, physiological needs present themselves in different ways. For example, an employee's need for a fair wage serves as the basis of job satisfaction and the lack of a fair salary becomes a deprivation need, often one that impedes that individual's ability to function as an engaged member of the team.

Safety needs are also basic to human survival and generally include those needs associated with a safe environment, but can also relate to financial security, job security and health and well-being. Employees need to feel safe not only physically, but with financial security and organizational structure as well. Once an individual has met their core needs for human survival, psychological needs take priority.

Psychological Needs

The next two stages on Maslow's Hierarchy relate to relationships, where individuals desire a sense of belonging and esteem or accomplishment. Belonging represents a need for individuals to form bonds with others, including being a part of a group, having friends, intimacy and trust. Failure to form these bonds can manifest itself in a number of ways including depression and suicidal thoughts. In the work setting, failure to form bonds can lead to employee dissatisfaction and turnover.

Esteem needs, are also psychological needs and include the desire for reputation or respect from others as well as seeing the value in oneself, often known as self-esteem. Maslow theorized that there are two types of esteem, a lower version indicating the need for respect from others, and higher esteem which includes the recognition of one's own value. Each type of esteem is important, but the theory contends that recognizing one's own value is of greater benefit when achieving satisfaction. By creating a culture of respect, organizations can support employee esteem needs and help them find their own value.

Self-Actualization

At the top of Maslow's pyramid is self-actualization, the desire an individual has for self-fulfillment, and to become the best version of themselves. Unlike the previous four levels, self-actualization does not come from the need to fulfill a deficit; rather self-actualization comes from motivation for personal growth. A self-actualized employee is internally motivated to grow and advance within an organization. Supporting the lower levels of Maslow's Hierarchy is the first step to creating self-actualized employees. As those needs are met, employers should focus on intrinsic motivation and self-determination. Focusing on providing meaningful work, recognition and growth can intrinsically motivate employees to reach their own self-determined career goals.

Application of Maslow's Hierarchy Theory

Providers

The need to improve physician satisfaction has become more pronounced as the United States faces a shortage of primary care physicians. Provider burn out and decreased job satisfaction of physicians is more prevalent among physicians than other U.S. workers (Shanafelt et al., 2012) and can negatively affect quality of care, healthcare costs, and patient safety. (Wallace, Lemaire and Ghalim, 2009) Research shows that providers that employ more components of HIT, with particular emphasis on e-prescribing (Jariwala et al., 2013) have a higher level of satisfaction (Elderet al., 2010).

There are several factors in the health care industry that can affect provider satisfaction both positively and negatively. Most notably, the Medicare Access and CHIP Reauthorization Act of 2015 (MACRA) moves physician Medicare compensation from a fee-for-service concept, to a merit-based incentive program. This significant change in fee structure can affect the most basic of needs of physicians in the United States. Fears of financial insecurity could result in an unmet safety need, and inhibit providers from reaching higher levels of satisfaction.

Staff

Much like providers, staff including Registered Nurses (RN) suffer from a higher level of burnout and lower job satisfaction than other jobs in the United States (Boamah, Read and Spence Laschinger, 2017); work environment as well as high nurse to patient ratios are often cited as a major factor for nurse retention issues. These retention issues have led to a shortage of RNs, which has plagued the United States for many years (Snavely, 2016).

A key component of the realization of psychological need fulfillment is for an individual to feel as though they are respected for their work and have the ability to communicate freely. Nurses who are not supported in their work environment may not feel as though this need is fulfilled, and therefore they cannot become highly satisfied employees.

Patients

The Affordable Care Act (ACA) moved the degree to which patients are satisfied with their care from an interesting number to track to an essential score that can impact the financial viability of healthcare organizations. Since physicians are measured both objectively and subjectively, the use of patient satisfaction surveys has increased and the weight attached to online ranking has become significant (Cohen, Myckatyn and Brandt, 2017). These core competencies as well as clinical quality measures can be applied using Maslow's Hierarchy of Needs. Clinical quality measures provide an overview of the degree to which patients' basic needs are being met (i.e. are they being provided for appropriately and safely?). This area of satisfaction has long been the focus of healthcare providers. However, in order for a patient to become satisfied, their psychological needs must be met as well.

Psychological needs have no physical manifestations so the only way to measure a patient's sense of belonging and esteem is by using a survey such as the Hospital Consumer Assessment of Healthcare Providers and Systems (HCAHPS). The core competencies of this instrument are most closely aligned with the feelings of lower level esteem as they relate to feeling respected and valued. Hospitals that are responsive to patients and communicate effectively can meet these psychological needs and improve satisfaction.

WHAT IS HCAHPS?

HCAHPS is a patient satisfaction survey and data collection methodology that is required by the Centers for Medicare and Medicaid Services for most hospitals in the United States. The HCAHPS surveys a random sample of adult patients after discharge (between 48 hours and six weeks) and asks them questions about their recent hospital stay including hospital experiences. These core questions revolve around communication, responsiveness of staff, hospital environment, pain management, medication communication and discharge instructions (CMS.gov, 2018).

Herzberg's Two-Factor Theory

Herzberg's Two-Factor Theory is a tool to measure job satisfaction and the motivation of employees. Fredrick Herzberg theorized that job satisfaction and dissatisfaction are two constructs that act independently of each other (Herzberg, 1964). Much like Maslow's Hierarchy, the Two-Factor Theory postulates that individuals are not satisfied if only their lower order needs (i.e. salary levels, safety and acceptable work conditions) are met. Rather, employees seek higher level psychological factors (i.e. achievement, recognition, and the value in the work itself) to be satisfied. One distinguishing difference between Maslow's Hierarchy and the Two-Factor Theory is that one set of job characteristics causes satisfaction (motivators) and another set causes job dissatisfaction (hygiene factors).

Motivators

Motivators refer to the positive satisfaction arising from the intrinsic characteristics of a job such as recognition for an achievement, challenging work, the opportunity to do something meaningful and a sense of importance to the organization. The presence of these factors serve as motivators and improve job satisfaction. However, Herzberg believed that the lack of these work characteristics do not cause dissatisfaction; rather, they suppress motivation and inhibit job satisfaction.

Hygiene

Hygiene factors are those variables external to the actual work itself and include things like pay, company policies, work conditions and supervision. While hygiene factors do not foster satisfaction or positively motivate employees, their absence creates dissatisfaction and inhibits motivation. Herzberg believed that it was important to improve hygiene factors and remove dissatisfaction before improving motivating factors to create satisfaction (Figure 3.2).

Application of Herzberg's Two-Factor Theory

Job Satisfaction

The Two-Factor Theory applies to the job satisfaction of a variety of professions including physicians and nurses. Research has shown that healthcare

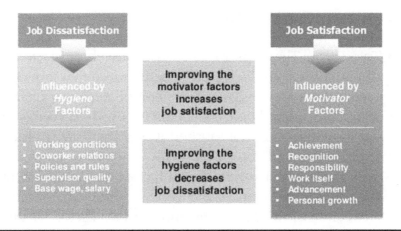

Figure 3.2   Herzberg's Two-Factor Principles.

professionals tend to be motivated by intrinsic factors, such as pride, appreciation and respect. Other motivating factors such as job attributes and co-workers have also been documented as motivational factors in doctors and nurses. Contrary to the Two-Factor Theory, a study of doctors, dentists and nurses found that pay was a motivator as opposed to a hygiene factor (Lambrou, Kontodimopoulos and Niakas, 2010).

Patient Satisfaction

The Two-Factor Theory has not been heavily used as a gauge for patient satisfaction, but some of the motivational and hygiene factors are present in the HCAHPS survey. Specifically, the HCAHPS asks questions regarding hospital environment including cleanliness, noise levels, pain management and assistance using bathroom facilities. These three factors are similar to hygiene factors identified by Herzberg, which could lead to dissatisfaction and thus negative patient satisfaction. Similarly, questions on the HCAHPS relate to Herzberg's motivating factors including provider's courtesy and respect, as well as their ability to explain discharge instructions.

How HIT Can Help

Providers

When first implemented, HIT received mixed reviews from physicians. Over time, as providers have accepted the workflow changes and new processes, provider satisfaction with HIT tools has improved (de Veer and Francke,

2010). The most prominent and widely used HIT tool is the EHR. The EHR serves as the backbone for almost all HIT tools. Research shows that provider satisfaction with the EHR is positively associated with improvements in information quality, increased access to real-time patient information and increased productivity (Nguyen, Bellucci and Nguyen, 2014).

E-prescribing is arguably the most well received HIT tool by providers. Providers have expressed satisfaction with e-prescribing ability to reduce after hour calls (Duffy et al., 2010) and improve physician efficiency (Parv et al., 2016). The reduction in medication related errors as a result of e-prescribing is also a significant satisfier (Hodgkinson et al., 2017).

Staff

Research shows that nurses have high rates of satisfaction with EHRs (Nguyen, Bellucci and Nguyen, 2014), but their satisfaction with HIT is not necessarily immediate. CPOE systems for example, impose significant changes on the workflow of physicians and nurses and can initially disrupt worker productivity. Research, however, shows that nurses' satisfaction with CPOE increases significantly once the nurses become comfortable with the new CPOE integrated workflow processes, typically one year after the CPOE system was implemented (Hoonakker et al., 2013).

Patients

Patient Portals provide patients access to their medical records including lab results and physician notes. This access to information supports patient engagement in their own care, providing a sense of belonging (Goldzweig et al., 2013). In this same regard, the use of social media and online groups like "Patients Like Me" can provide significant satisfaction as they provide the same sense of belonging and feelings of connectedness.

How Health Information Technology Impacts Satisfaction Results from the STEPS™ Value Collection

Provider

An evaluation of the HIMSS STEPS™ collection of value statements and data reveals that "improving provider work-life balance" and "preventing provider burnout" are frequently cited benefits of HIT. HIT offers providers many tools to increase satisfaction and reduce burnout by empowering physicians to manage their own time. Each of the HIT tools in these cases have a significant impact on improving provider satisfaction, principally by improving their quality of life, by enabling better work-life balance.

> I can review 50 labs on a Saturday while I'm doing the laundry. I review my labs online, and if I find someone needs to go to the hospital right away, I pick up the phone and call them. If it's a problem that we need to address within 48 hours, I'll put an alert message on my system, so that the person automatically gets a telephone call or an email.
>
> **Karen Smith, MD**
> *FAAFP (Atwal PMS, 2011)*

Staff

The HIMSS STEPS™ Database includes 176 cases citing staff satisfaction as a benefit of HIT. The most frequently referenced tool in these case studies was the EMR, with "improvements in workflow" the most often cited HIT benefit, followed by "reduction in wait time for orders" and "results assisted in providing appropriate and timely care."

Non-clinical staff also benefit from HIT implementations, especially as it relates to workflow issues. Improvements in the movement of patients through care settings (e.g. physician office) is associated with improved staff morale. Staff members also tend to have a greater sense of empowerment in making decisions when they have access to data needed to make certain decisions.

> Clinical staff can run reports themselves, and the system is easy enough to use, so anyone can do it. It has really helped us along with our quality initiatives.
>
> **Michele Lagana**
> *CFO, CIO Baltimore Medical System (Azara Healthcare, 2016)*

Patients

The stakeholder group with the most documented case studies in the HIMSS STEPS™ Database involving satisfaction are "patients." The STEPS™

Database has 569 patient satisfaction examples in which value was derived from health information technology. "Patient convenience" and "improved communications" are the most commonly identified benefits in these examples, with other frequently cited benefits including "ready access to medical records including lab results," "ease of prescription refills," "reduced wait times," and "using telehealth to connect to providers." Of interest, "reduced patient wait times" was specifically mentioned as a patient satisfier 115 times in the database, demonstrating the extent to which HIT can improve the patient experience. Communication with providers using specific HIT tools, such as "telehealth" and the "patient portal," were also mentioned as drivers of patient satisfaction.

> This generation that we're in today, predominantly the mom and dad in the pediatric world, definitely are mobile savvy and mobile aware. They want to have their information, and they want to have it now. So we feel that the engagement from that perspective— getting them engaged that early on—will get us a much better outcome earlier because they like the idea of being engaged on mobile and not face-to-face. They don't like the face-to-face. They like texting, and they like to look it up on a handheld.

Eric McCann
Chief Information Officer, Miami Children's, 2015

Summary

Satisfaction is an important consideration for all healthcare executives and managers. The use of HIT to address the basic as well as higher order needs of providers, staff and patients has grown in number and sophistication. The use of the technologies to produce satisfaction among providers, staff and patients is prevalent and apparent in the HIMSS STEPS™ Database.

Discussion Questions

1. Recreate the Maslow's Hierarchy of Need triangle and include at least two of the value comments from the HIMSS STEPS™ Database. Explain.

2. How is HIT helping providers, staff and patients reach levels of Maslow's Hierarchy?

3. Using the value comments, explain how the Herzberg Two-Factor Theory is affected by HIT tools.

4. Align the HCAHPS survey with the either the Herzberg Two-Factor Theory or Maslow's Hierarchy of Needs. Explain your results.

5. How do each of the HIT tools improve provider, staff and patient satisfaction?

References

Atwal PMS. EHR System Helps Improve the Quality of Care for Patients: An Interview with Dr. Karen Smith. https://www.healthit.gov/buzz-blog/ehr-case-studies/ehr-system-improves-quality-care-patients/. Posted 11/9/2011.

Azara Healthcare. Azara Baltimore Case Study. https://azarahealthcare.com/wp-content/.../07/Azara-Baltimore-Case-Study-view.pdf. Posted 7/2016.

Boamah SA, Read EA, and Spence Laschinger HK. Factors influencing new graduate nurse burnout development, job satisfaction and patient care quality: A time-lagged study. *Journal of Advanced Nursing.* 2017;73(5):1182–1195. doi:10.1111/jan.13215.

CMS.gov. HCAHPS: Patients' Perspectives of Care Survey https://www.cms.gov/Medicare/Quality-Initiatives-Patient-Assessment-Instruments/HospitalQualityInits/HospitalHCAHPS.html. Posted 12/12/18.

Cohen JB, Myckatyn TM and Brandt K. The importance of patient satisfaction: A blessing, a curse, or simply irrelevant? *Plastic And Reconstructive Surgery.* 2017;139(1):257–261. doi:10.1097/PRS.0000000000002848.

de Veer AJE and Francke AL. Attitudes of nursing staff toward electronic patient records: A questionnaire survey. *International Journal of Nursing Studies.* 2010;47(7):846–854. doi:10.1016/j.ijnurstu.2009.11.016.

Duffy RL, Yiu SSA, Molokhia E, Walker R and Perkins RA. Effects of electronic prescribing on the clinical practice of a family medicine residency. *Family Medicine.* 2010;42(5):358–363.

Elder KT, Wiltshire JC, Rooks RN, Belue R and Gary LC. Health information technology and physician career satisfaction. *Perspectives In Health Information Management.* 2010;7.

Goldzweig C, Orshansky G, Paige NM et al. Electronic patient portals: Evidence on health outcomes, satisfaction, efficiency, and attitudes: A systematic review. *Annals of Internal Medicine.* 2013;159(10):677–687. doi:10.7326/0003-4819-159-10-201311190-00006.

Herzberg F. Motivation: Hygiene concept and problems of manpower. *Personnel Administration.* 1964;27:3–7.

Hodgkinson MR, Larmour I, Lin S, Stormont AJ, Paul E. The impact of an inte-grated electronic medication prescribing and dispensing system on prescribing and dispensing errors: A before and after study. *Journal of Pharmacy Practice & Research.* 2017;47(2):110–120. doi:10.1002/jppr.1243.

Hoonakker PLT, Carayon P and Brown RL. Changes in end-user satisfaction with computerized provider order entry over time among nurses and providers in intensive care units. *Journal of the American Medical Informatics Association.* 2013;20(2):252–259. doi:10.1136/amiajnl-2012-001114.

Jariwala KS, Holmes ER, Banahan BF and McCaffrey DJ. Research brief: Adoption of and experience with e-prescribing by primary care physicians. *Research in Social and Administrative Pharmacy.* 2013;9:120–128. doi:10.1016/j.sapharm.2012.04.003.

Lambrou P, Kontodimopoulos N, Niakas D. Motivation and job satisfaction among medical and nursing staff in a Cyprus public general hospital. *Human Resources for Health,* 2010;8:26. doi:10.1186/1478-4491-8-26.

Maslow AH. A Theory of Human Motivation. *Psychological Review.* 1943;50 (4), 430–437.

McCann E. CIO one-on-one: patient engagement. www.healthcareitnews.com/news/cio-one-one-patient-engagement. Posted 2015.

Nguyen L, Bellucci E and Nguyen LT. Electronic health records implementa-tion: An evaluation of information system impact and contingency factors. *International Journal of Medical Informatics.* 2014;83(11):779–796.

Parv L, Kruus P, Mõtte K, Ross P and Mõtte K. An evaluation of e-prescribing at a national level. *Informatics for Health & Social Care.* 2016;41(1):78–95. doi:10.310 9/17538157.2014.948170.

Shanafelt TD, Boone S, Tan L et al. Burnout and satisfaction with work-life balance among US physicians relative to the general U.S. population. *Arch Intern Med.* 2012; 172(18):1377–1385.

Snavely TM. Data Watch. A brief economic analysis of the looming nursing short-age in the United States. *Nursing Economics.* 2016;34(2):98–100.

Wallace JE, Lemaire JB, Ghali WA. Physician wellness: A missing qual-ity indicator. *Lancet.* 14 November, 2009;374:97021714–1721. doi:10.1016/S0140-6736(09)61424-0.

Chapter 4

Treatment/Clinical

Lorren Pettit

Learning Objectives

- Identify and define at least one significant challenge evidence-based medicine addresses for clinicians.
- Describe the sub-values of the Treatment/Clinical domain.
- Assess the role HIT can play in addressing the clinical quality goals of external regulatory bodies.

Definitions

- *Clinical decision-making process*: A contextual, continuous, and evolving process, in which data are gathered, interpreted and evaluated in order to select an evidence-based choice of action (Tiffen, Corbridge and Slimmer, 2014).
- *Clinical Decision Support System (CDSS)*: An application that uses pre-established rules and guidelines that can be created and edited by the healthcare organization and integrates clinical data from several sources to generate alerts and treatment suggestions.
- *Evidenced-based medicine*: The conscientious, explicit, judicious and reasonable use of modern, best evidence in making decisions about the care of an individual. It integrates clinical experience and patient values with best available research information. Evidence-based medicine

follows four steps: formulate a clear clinical question from a patient's problem; search the literature for relevant clinical articles; evaluate (critically appraise) the evidence for its validity and usefulness; and implement useful findings in clinical practice (HIMSS, 2017).

■ *Quality of care*: Degrees of excellence of care in relation to actual medical knowledge, identified by quality tracers based on outcomes of care, as well as on structure and process (HIMSS, 2017).

■ *Patient safety*: The prevention of errors and adverse effects to patients associated with healthcare. While healthcare has become more effective, it has also become more complex, with greater use of new technologies, medicines and treatments (World Health Organization, n.d.).

■ *Quality Payment Program (QPP)*: The QPP established under the Medicare Access and CHIP Reauthorization Act of 2015 (MACRA), was created as a means to reimburse participating providers (physicians) with the main goals to (CMS, 2016):
  – Improve health outcomes
  – Spend wisely
  – Minimize burden of participation
  – Be fair and transparent

■ *Outcome measure*: A parameter for evaluating the health state of a patient (or change in health status) resulting from healthcare—desirable or adverse (CMS, 2016).

■ *Intermediate outcome*: Refers to a change produced by a healthcare intervention that leads to a longer term outcome (e.g. a reduction in blood pressure is an intermediate outcome that leads to a reduction in the risk of longer term outcomes such as cardiac infarction or stroke) (CMS, 2016).

Introduction

The second domain of the STEPS™ Framework, Treatment/Clinical, is arguably the most critical domain in the STEPS™ Framework. Intimately tied to a healthcare provider's core business, this domain focuses on the positive impact of HIT to facilitate *patient care interventions* (treatment) and enhance *patient outcomes* (clinical) regardless of the care setting. Drilling down further into these headers reveals the treatment and clinical benefits of HIT within the following two sub-domains:

■ *Quality of care* reflects clinical outcomes
■ *Patient Safety* and *Efficiencies* reflect treatment procedures

Finally, though the STEPS™ Framework represents this beneficial domain by highlighting the "T" of "treatment," this does not suggest *treatment* benefits have a greater priority than *clinical* benefits. Both beneficial manifestations are important.

Foundational Elements

The widespread delivery of safe, effective and affordable healthcare has long challenged clinicians and provider organizations the world over. In the United States, the healthcare delivery system has been marked by "underuse, overuse, misuse, and variation in use" (AHRQ, 1998). While the reasons surrounding the genesis and sustainability of this situation are numerous and complex, one factor of particular interest to this chapter involves the clinical decision-making process.

Experience and learning have long guided physicians in the selection of interventions designed to yield the best outcomes possible for their patients. Yet, variances in experience and learning could lead physicians to pursue remarkably different interventions when presented with the same symptoms and conditions. Indeed, the explosive growth of medical research and knowledge has aided in the proliferation of practice variations (and outcomes) as it is impossible for physicians to stay abreast of the latest therapies and medical advances. For example, to keep up on published randomized controlled trials (the gold standard of clinical research) for just the ten most common diagnoses in a field, physicians would need to read 12 peer reviewed publications per week (Byyny, 2012).

The process of thoroughly searching the world's research literature and appraising the quality and relevance of studies identified requires skills and training most clinicians do not possess and is frankly unsustainable. Fortunately, two significant developments have emerged and converged to aid in usurping the opinion-based clinical decision-making and patient management approach:

1. Evidenced-based medicine (EBM)
2. Computers

Evidence-Based Medicine

The past few decades have witnessed healthcare organizations investing heavily in the development of evidence-based clinical guidelines to improve the consistency and safety of patient care interventions. At its core, EBM reflects the integration of best available research evidence with clinical judgment (i.e. the clinician's accumulated experience, knowledge and clinical skills) as applied to the care of individual patients (i.e. the patient's values and preferences). Reflecting the standard of clinical practice taught to new clinicians, EBM adherence is increasingly used to measure a provider's quality of care.

Computers

The effective dissemination of EBM guidelines is a challenging task. Information technologies have emerged as an effective means to assist in the integration of guidelines into clinical practice (Burstin, 2008). Not only do they provide ready access to a vast array of medical information (via the Internet), but CDSS for example, combine an evidence-based database with a smart search engine tool allowing clinicians to more rapidly survey the evidence and determine how to apply the information to their patient.

Treatment/Clinical Improvement Measures and MIPS

One significant resource to reference when measuring the quality of care delivered by a clinician involves the quality measures category of the Centers for Medicare and Medicaid (CMS) Merit-Based Incentive Program. The Merit-Based Incentive Payment System (MIPS) is a payment mechanism for providers (e.g. physicians). The program combines all Medicare pay for performance programs (Meaningful Use, Value-Based Modifier and the Physician Quality Reporting System) under one umbrella. Providers opting to participate in MIPS agree to have their Medicare Part B payment amounts annually adjusted based on their performance in four categories:

1. Quality Payment Program (QPP)
2. Resource use
3. Clinical practice improvement activities and
4. Meaningful Use of an EHR system

Providers earn points in each of these four categories with 100 being the maximum combined number of points one is able to earn in a calendar year. The number of points providers earn annually determines their Medicare payment rate for the coming year. Performance in the QPP is the most heavily weighted of the four categories, contributing up to 60% of a provider's MIPS Final Score in 2017.

The QPP is relevant to the STEPS™ Treatment/Clinical sub-domains because QPP lists over 270 measures from which providers can select measures to demonstrate their clinical quality performance. Arguably, HIT can be used to facilitate the clinical outcomes of many of these measures, and, therefore provides a valuable gauge for assessing the impact of HIT on clinical performance.

Sub-Domain: Quality of Care

Of the 270+ quality measures in QPP from which providers can select the basis for their QPP score, just over one-quarter are classified as *outcome* or *intermediate outcome* measures. As such, these measures reflect the clinical quality of care outcomes of interest to CMS, and by extension, the quality of care sub-domain within the STEPS™ Treatment/Clinical framework. Examples of outcome measures that could positively benefit from the introduction of HIT in the intervention include the following:

1. *HIV viral load suppression*: The percentage of patients, regardless of age, with a diagnosis of HIV with an HIV viral load less than 200 copies/mL at last HIV viral load test during the measurement year.
2. *Quality of life assessment for patients with primary headache disorders*: Percentage of patients with a diagnosis of primary headache disorder whose health related quality of life (HRQoL) was assessed with a tool(s) during at least two visits during the 12 month measurement period and whose health related quality of life score stayed the same or improved.
3. *All-cause hospital readmission measure*: The 30-day all-cause hospital readmission measure is a risk-standardized readmission rate for beneficiaries age 65 or older who were hospitalized at a short-stay acute care hospital and experienced an unplanned readmission for any cause to an acute care hospital within 30 days of discharge. Applies only to groups of 16 or more eligible clinicians.

Examples of *intermediate outcome measures*, which could benefit from the use of HIT, include the following:

■ *Controlling high blood pressure (See also the HEDIS measure with slightly different criteria)*: Percentage of patients 18–85 years of age who had a diagnosis of hypertension and whose blood pressure was adequately controlled (<140/90 mmHg) during the measurement period.

■ *Adherence to antipsychotic medications for individuals with schizophrenia*: Percentage of individuals at least 18 years of age as of the beginning of the measurement period with schizophrenia or schizoaffective disorder who had at least two prescriptions filled for any antipsychotic medication and who had a proportion of days covered (PDC) of at least 0.8 for antipsychotic medications during the measurement period (12 consecutive months).

CASE #4.1 QUALITY OF CARE CASE EXAMPLE— HIV VIRAL LOAD SUPPRESSION

While it is possible for the clinical outcome and treatment process measures to be positively impacted without the aid of HIT, the HIMSS STEPS™ Framework is interested in quantifying how the use of HIT positively impacts these measures. Arguably, changes in the pre- post- HIT implementation performance on these measures should reflect the impact of HIT in each situation.

To illustrate the potential role HIT could play in benefiting QPP measures, we can consider the HIV viral load suppression measure noted above. HIV viral load suppression is a population measure reflecting the number of people living with HIV who are receiving a drug therapy designed to completely stop the virus from reproducing and have a low presence of HIV in their blood.* Epidemiologists are interested in this measure because the drug therapy (commonly referred to as antiretroviral therapy or ART) is known to prevent further damage to one's immune system, tends to decrease AIDS-associated deaths, allows for one's immune function to return to normal, and reduces the risk of transmitting

---

* www.who.int/healthinfo/indicators/2015/chi_2015_87_hiv_viral_load.pdf

HIV infection to others.* The inclusion of this measure in CMS' QPP is significant as it supports the 2010 National HIV/AIDS Strategy (NHAS).[†] More specifically, the NHAS contains targets to increase the proportion of all HIV-infected individuals in the USA who are aware of their status in terms of having detectable antibodies to HIV in their blood, to be linked to care within 3 months of diagnosis, continuously engaged in HIV care, and ultimately achieve suppression of the virus. Unfortunately, there is a wide array of barriers challenging individuals in optimally engaging in their care (e.g. lack of housing, lack of insurance, etc.). Evidence suggests a combination of individual and system-level interventions have the potential to improve care engagement and the quality of HIV medical and support services.[‡§]

In attempting to expand the body of evidence concerning effective interventions, researchers in one study explored the effect HIT had on comprehensive care services, patient engagement in HIV care, and viral suppression.[¶] In their study, the researchers analyzed the performance of six healthcare organizations designated as a HIT intervention demonstration sites. These sites leveraged HIT to primarily enhance (1) utilization of comprehensive care services (preventative screenings; utilization of support services), or (2) patient engagement in their care (linkage to patient compliance databases; proactive lab and pharmacy ordering systems).

The specific HIT interventions employed by the organizations varied by organization:

* Factors associated with HIV viral load suppression on antiretroviral therapy in Vietnam.Suresh Rangarajan, Donn J Colby, Le Truong Giang, Duc Duong Bui, Huu Hung Nguyen, Plui Broh Tou, Tran Tri Danh, Ngoc Bao Chau Tran, Duc Anh Nguyen, Bao Tram Hoang Nguyen, Vu Tuyet Nga Doan, Nhat Quang Nguyen, Van Phuoc Pham, Duc Giang Dao, Mario Chen, Yanwu Zeng, Thi Thu Van Tieu, My Hanh Tran, Thi Hoa Le, Xuan Chien Hoang, Gary West, J Virus Erad. 2016 Apr; 2(2): 94–101. Published online 1 April, 2016. www.ncbi.nlm.nih.gov/pmc/articles/PMC4965252/.

† Office of National AIDS Policy. National HIV/AIDS Strategy for the United States. 2010. www.cdc. gov/hiv/pdf/research/demonstration/echpp/reports/nhas.pdf.

‡ Mugavero MJ. Improving engagement in HIV care: What can we do? *Top HIV Med.* 2008;16:156–161.

§ Mugavero MJ Norton WE and Saag MS. Health care system and policy factors influencing engagement in HIV medical care: piecing together the fragments of a fractured health care delivery system. *Clin Infect Dis.* 2011;52(Suppl 2):S238–S246.

¶ Shade SB, Steward WT, Koester KA, Chakravarty D and Myers JJ. Health information technology interventions enhance care completion, engagement in HIV care and treatment, and viral suppression among HIV-infected patients in publicly funded settings. *J Am Med Inform Assoc.* April 2015;22(e1):e104-11. doi: 10.1136/amiajnl-2013-002623. Epub July 16, 2014.

■ Use of an EHR with summary comparison reports shared across area health service providers. This shared record helped providers develop targeted prevention services, and create health record alerts to identify and intervene with patients who had not received needed clinical services.

■ Use of a structured patient summary within the organization's EHR that included highlighted alerts to identify needed clinical services. By targeting "high need patients," defined as patients who had detectable viral loads despite multiple medical and social support service visits across multiple social service providers, this approach provided case managers with access to these patient summaries to facilitate coordination of support services and reinforce engagement in HIV care. This approach assumed that coordination of care would result in utilization of fewer redundant support services.

■ Access for support service providers to a regional medical center EHR to facilitate coordination of support services and reinforce engagement in HIV care.

■ Creation of continuity of care patient summaries made available to patients through a patient portal to facilitate engagement in HIV care.

■ Linkage of data from the state patient compliance database to EHRs in publicly funded health facilities so that alerts would fire whenever a patient known to be out-of-care for HIV presented for services in an emergency room and other (non-HIV) healthcare settings. Providers at the care site then acted on the alert to facilitate the patient's re-engagement in HIV care.

■ Implementation of an automatic electronic laboratory ordering and prescribing system to reduce the time needed to access these services and to enhance engagement in HIV care.

Researchers in this study observed a statistically significant improvement in outcome measures directly targeted by the HIT intervention(s) in five of the six demonstration sites. For example, using patient surveillance data to identify out-of-care individuals, resulted in patient engagement increasing from 65% to 83%, and the proactive use of an automatic electronic laboratory ordering and prescribing system resulted in prescribed antiretroviral therapy usage increasing from 73% to 92%. Moreover, five of the six demonstration sites showed a statistically significant increase in undetectable viral load with the proportion of patients with an undetectable viral load at one site increasing from a 53% to 68%.* Commenting on their findings, the researchers noted that to meaningfully change outcomes, clinicians must utilize the information received, arguing that an HIT system appears to be most successful at altering HIV patient engagement when it is paired with quality improvement goals that are specifically tied to linkage and retention outcomes.

Sub-Domain: Patient Safety

The second sub-domain, *Patient Safety*, involves treatment interventions designed to ensure patients are free from harm during the delivery of care.

The issue of patient safety was elevated in the national dialogue when the Institute of Medicine (IOM) released its seminal publication "To Err Is Human: Building a Safer Health System" in 1999. Equating the number of deaths each year in U.S. hospitals due to medical errors to a jumbo airplane crashing each day for a year, the IOM powerfully challenged healthcare providers to aggressively address medical errors in the treatment of patients.

The use of HIT has been presented as one of the solutions healthcare providers could leverage to diminish medical errors from occurring. HIT plays a role in patient safety in a myriad of ways; from ensuring clinicians have ready access to clinical decision support tools, to medication reminders and drug-to-drug interaction alerts. Information technologies support healthcare workers by assisting in tasks that require the accurate interpretation of data. CDSS for example, provide evidence-based insights in the context of specific patient data through a myriad of ways, to include:

■ *Alerts and reminders*: A CDSS will alert a clinician when certain inputted data is alarming or a potential risk to the patient. For example, if a patient has a history of cardiac issues and the system reads that their blood pressure is abnormally high, it can alert the clinician of the abnormality.

---

* https://academic.oup.com/jamia/article/22/e1/e104/700744

■ *Diagnostic assistance*: Patient data can be compared to an external knowledge base in order to present possible diagnoses. This is beneficial when the clinician is not confident with his or her knowledge on a certain condition, when there is new medical knowledge on a condition, or when the patient's symptoms are complex or seemingly unrelated.

■ *Prescription decision support*: a prescribing decision support system (PDSS) can check for drug-to-drug interactions, dosage errors, and drug contraindications such as patient allergies.

■ *Image recognition and interpretation*: Systems are now capable of interpreting clinical images ranging from simple X-rays to MRIs or CT scans. Perhaps the greatest benefits occur when the system examines a series of images over time and detects minute changes that may have been overlooked by a professional due to the minuteness of the detail.

As with the previous *quality of care* discussion, providers can look to the CMS QPP to identify *patient safety* performance measures which could be positively impacted by HIT. Below are three examples of such measures:

■ *Appropriate treatment for children with upper respiratory infection (URI)*: Percentage of children 3 months through 18 years of age who were diagnosed with URI and were not dispensed an antibiotic prescription on or within three days after the episode.

■ *Falls—risk assessment*: Percentage of patients aged 65 years and older with a history of falls who had a risk assessment for falls completed within 12 months.

■ *Evaluation or interview for risk of opioid misuse*: All patients 18 and older prescribed opiates for longer than six weeks duration evaluated for risk of opioid misuse using a brief validated instrument (e.g. Opioid Risk Tool, SOAAP-R) or patient interview documented at least once during Opioid Therapy in the medical record.

CASE #4.2: PATIENT SAFETY CASE EXAMPLE

Mission Hospital in Asheville, North Carolina, offers an excellent example of technology supporting the patient safety measure related to patient falls. Though the hospital had instituted a multicomponent fall-prevention program to include adherence to a number of standard fall-prevention interventions (e.g. bed locked in low position with rails up), the neuroscience unit leaders believed their overall falls rate (5.74 per 1000 patient-days of care) could be significantly reduced. Working with a large HIT vendor, Mission Health implemented a three-month pilot study to evaluate the impact of "virtual sitter" technology as an alternative to qualified staff sitters in patients' rooms. Unit leaders used infrared cameras to sense full-body 3-D patient movements under any ambient light. When a patient's movements generated a virtual sitter alert, the monitor technician intervened

During the three-month pilot, 98 "high-risk" patients were monitored using the virtual sitter system. Of the control group patients, no one experienced unassisted falls and no one reported injuries by the end of the pilot study. All other patients on the neuroscience unit experienced an unassisted fall rate of 4.06 and an injury rate of 2.45 per 1000 patient-days of care. Analysis showed that verbal redirection alone (accounting for 50% of all virtual sitter interventions during the pilot) was highly effective in keeping the patient in their beds or chairs. This finding was significant because the verbal redirection helped to prevent falls and injuries and prevented the interruption of nurses from their other duties. (Westle, Burkert and Paulus, 2017).

Sub-Domain: Efficiencies

The third and final sub-domain under the Treatment/Clinical banner, Efficiencies, involves treatment interventions designed to ensure clinicians are expending minimal resources to realize maximum results. Identified by the Institute of Medicine in its 2001 publication "Crossing the quality chasm" as one of the six characteristics of high-quality healthcare, efficiency is admittedly difficult to quantify. Though measures of healthcare efficiency are reported in the literature and advocated by consultants, health policy experts, accreditation agencies, employers, and payers, there is limited agreement on the relationship between cost and quality.

The lack of agreement surrounding efficiency calculations should not discourage its use as evidence of the benefit of HIT. It is still possible to argue that certain interventions can yield efficiencies in treatment without achieving universal agreement on the data inputs/outputs.

In keeping with the previous sections as to the measures providers may want to look toward to impact through the use of HIT, below are two examples of efficiency measures from the QPP list:

- *Overuse of neuroimaging for patients with primary headache and a normal neurological examination*: Percentage of patients with a diagnosis of primary headache disorder for whom advanced brain imaging was not ordered.
- *Age appropriate screening colonoscopy*: The percentage of patients greater than 85 years of age who received a screening colonoscopy from January 1 to December 31.

Efficiencies Case Example

A study by Guiriguet et al. (2016) in Spain underscores the efficiencies of appropriately screening individuals for colonoscopies, per the QPP measure noted above. Recognized as having the highest incident rate of all cancers, colorectal cancer can be effectively addressed when screened in populations that are at average risk of developing the disease. The European guidelines for quality assurance in colorectal cancer-screening states that the participation rate represents a key quality indicator for ensuring effectiveness and efficiency of population-based screening programs. However, participation in screening programs in Spain were not reaching the recommended rates. To address this challenge, researchers at the Catalan Health Institute in Spain studied the impact electronic alerts/reminders in primary care EMR's might have on participation in an organized colorectal cancer-screening program. The results of the study found that electronic reminders for individuals with a follow-up meeting with their primary care physician resulted in an 11% increase in screening participation (Guiriguet et al., 2016).

Conclusion

Intimately tied to a healthcare provider's core business, the Treatment/Clinical domain of the STEPS™ Framework is arguably the model's most critical domain. This domain focuses on the positive impact of IT to facilitate patient care interventions (treatment) and enhance patient outcomes (clinical). The role of HIT has gained in significance as a means to leverage EBM in addressing disparities in the use of best clinical practices and patient outcomes. While it is possible for organizations to positively address treatment and clinical goals (including QPP measures) without the aid of HIT, HIT can help facilitate clinicians in their practice so as to prescribe the best course of action to achieve optimal outcomes.

Discussion Questions

1. What are the major challenges/problems that EBM addresses for clinicians?
2. Do you agree that of all the values that are derived from the EHR, treatment and clinical quality improvements are the most important? Why/why not?
3. How does digital technology support reporting to external agencies, such as CMS, insurance companies, who require achievement of specified minimum quality measures?
4. Provide an example from your own experience in which the availability of an EHR aided in achieving a better outcome than would have been achieved if it had not been available.

CASE FOR DISCUSSION: NEBRASKA MEDICINE

Empowered by a vision to become the organization of choice for comprehensive care in their region, Nebraska Medicine is utilizing the technology available within their EHR to improve the overall health of patients. With over 1000 physicians and 50 specialty and primary care clinics in Omaha and the surrounding areas, Nebraska Medicine is one of the most esteemed academic health system in the region.

Nebraska Medicine had a 47% reduction in CAUTI rate and a 29% reduction in catheter days, as a result of their internal initiative focused on reducing CAUTIs. During June 2017, Nebraska Medicine had no CAUTIs across their system, as a result of the initiative's success. Nebraska Medicine saved $1.4 million by working toward the "Zero Harm" goal for cost reduction.

Source: HIMSS, 2017: Nebraska Medicine: Davies Enterprise Award.

DISCUSSION QUESTIONS

Nebraska Medicine defined a far-reaching vision for their future, and strategically used their EHR to help achieve their vision, as exemplified in the area of Clinical Improvement described in this case. In what other clinical areas might you expect to see improvement as a result of using digital technologies in achieving an organizational vision? In such a large organization, how would you go about getting the entire medical staff to buy-into the vision and the IT strategy? What other clinical treatment and outcome benefits might the organization and the community experience as a result of Nebraska Medicine's use of their EHR?

References

AHRQ. *The Challenge and Potential for Assuring Quality Health Care for the 21st Century.* 1998. Rockville, MD.

Burstin HR. Achieving the potential of health information technology. *Journal of General Internal Medicine.* 2008: 23(4), 502–504.

Byyny RL. The data deluge: The information explosion in medicine and science. *The Pharos.* 2012: 75(2), 2–5.

CMS. *Quality Measures Inventory User Guide and Data Dictionary.* Updated January 2016.

Guiriguet C, Muñoz-Ortiz L, Burón A, Rivero I, Grau J, Vela-Vallespín C, Vilarrubí M, et al. Alerts in electronic medical records to promote a colorectal cancer screening programme: a cluster randomised controlled trial in primary care. British Journal of General Practice. 2016: 66(648): e483–e490.

HIMSS. Nebraska Medicine: Davies Enterprise Award. 2017. www.himss.org/library/nebraska-medicine-davies-enterprise-award.

HIMSS. *HIMSS Dictionary of Health Information Technology Terms, Acronyms, and Organizations*, 4th Edition. 2017. Boca Raton, FL: Taylor & Francis Group.

Tiffen J, Corbridge SJ, Slimmer L. Enhancing clinical decision making: Development of a contiguous definition and conceptual framework. *Journal of Professional Nursing.* 2014: 399–405.

Westle M, Burkert G and Paulus R. Reducing inpatient falls by integrating new technology with workflow redesign. 2017. Retrieved from NEJM Catalyst: https://catalyst.nejm.org/reducing-inpatient-falls-virtual-sitter/.

World Health Organization. Patient safety. n.d. Retrieved from World Health Organization: Regional Office for Europe: www.euro.who.int/en/health-topics/Health-systems/patient-safety.

Chapter 5

Electronic Secure Data/Information

Margaret Schulte and Lee Kim

Learning Objectives

- Explain the role and value of data in the organizational context.
- Assess the ways in which electronic data in healthcare organizations provides value to the provider in clinical decision-making and to the patient.
- Identify the various groups or organizations who have an interest in healthcare data and the ways in which the EHR helps to serve their needs through data sharing and reporting.
- Describe how digital technology assists in ensuring the security of patient information.

Definitions

- *De-identified data*: A de-Identified data set is a data set that meets both of the following:
  - Does not identify any individual that is a subject of the data.
  - Does not provide any reasonable basis for identifying any individual that is a subject of the data (University of Michigan Medical School, 2016).

■ *Evidence-based medicine (EBM)*: EBM is the conscientious, explicit and judicious use of current best evidence in making decisions about the care of individual patients. The practice of EBM means integrating individual clinical expertise with the best available external clinical evidence from systematic research (New York University School of Medicine, 1996).

■ *Systems theory*: "Systems theory is an approach to organizations which likens the enterprise to an organism with interdependent parts, each with its own specific function and interrelated responsibilities" (Foster, 2012).

■ *Transitions of care*: "Transitions of care" refers to the movement of patients between health care locations, providers or different levels of care within the same location, as their conditions and care needs change" (NTOCC, 2018).

Introduction

In the study of organizational development, systems theory is fundamental. Organizations are social systems in which sub-systems come together to fulfill a mission and achieve the goals developed within the context of the mission. This is an essential concept to achieve management success. However, the challenge of systems management becomes particularly acute when an organization is "siloed" into numerous geographically dispersed and/or specialty sub-systems or units, each with a unique essential role in the functioning of the whole. Managers rely on "systems theory" for guiding principles in developing and sustaining their complex organizational structures, in reducing fragmentation, and in unifying their organization into an integrated, smoothly functioning whole.

Healthcare organizations are particularly complex in that they are comprised of a wide array of sub-units, many of which are highly specialized. In healthcare provider organizations, the sub-systems may include finance, diagnostic services, outpatient and emergency services, patient records/information management, IT and the specialty and general medical practices that are at the core of the organization. All of these sub-systems are interrelated within the management structures and policies that cause the sub-systems to work together to achieve goals they share in common. This is where systems theory applies in healthcare. As defined by Fisher, "systems theory is an approach to organizations which likens the enterprise to an organism with interdependent parts, each with its own specific function and interrelated responsibilities" (Fisher, 2012). Katz and Khan, who initially introduced systems theory to the organizational environment, posit that in systems theory inter-relatedness and interdependence of all parts of the organization must be recognized. They go on to suggest that the entity's success is, consequently, reliant on formal and informal communication throughout the organization (Katz and Khan, 1966–1967).

Communication is core to successful functioning of a system and its interrelated sub-systems. Communication, interpreted broadly, refers not only to interactions between human beings, but also to the substance of those communications. In healthcare, as in so many businesses, data and its analytical results are part of what is shared in the communications loop necessary to achieve performance improvement in clinical care, in financial results, and in each of the many sub-systems that make up the whole. In effect, the transformation of healthcare is only possible through the availability of data and the ability to share and communicate that data's acquisition and analysis throughout the system of care. In fact,

> The future of health care is being shaped dramatically by a number of significant trends. With the cost of care on the rise, the industry is experiencing a shift toward preventative and value-based care. At the same time, technologies like wearable devices, at-home testing services and telemedicine are empowering patients to be more engaged with, and proactive about, their own health. Meanwhile, the industry is grappling with the tension between encouraging data sharing to maximize the benefits of data and maintaining patient privacy and trust. All of these developments are altering the role of physicians and their relationships with patients. Behind these trends is one fundamental force driving health care transformation: the power of data.
>
> **Stanford Medicine, 2017**

The Value of Data in Healthcare

Well over 100 years ago, William Thomson, 1st Baron Kelvin (i.e. Lord Kelvin) identified numerical data as the cornerstone of successful science when he stated, "If you can not measure it, you can not improve it. …

When you measure it and express it in numbers, you know something about it" (Kelvin, 1883). In healthcare, in particular, data shares its position of importance with the many skilled human beings who interact directly with the patient. As data is digitized, it puts a powerful tool in the hands of clinicians to achieve performance improvement. The data and the clinician's expertise comprise a partnership for significant advances in the quality of clinical care.

The rapid transition from paper to electronic records in healthcare has created an enormous opportunity to derive value for the patient, the provider and the payer that could only be imagined just two decades earlier. The adoption of electronic systems has enabled the collection and sharing of data and, more importantly, the analysis of that data to inform clinical decision-making at the bedside, support clinical research, improve patient engagement, drive efficiency and cost savings into the system of care, and ultimately foster the transformation of healthcare delivery. Healthcare is inherently based on science (i.e. the science of medicine, the science of clinical research). In the last decade, healthcare has finally begun to gain access to the treasure trove of insight and information that patient care data represents. It drives EBM for better decision-making at the bedside. It also propels clinical research leading to new findings to improve clinical options to address individual and population health issues that have been heretofore, out of reach.

Electronic data and its related analytics, have come to be recognized as essential to improved medical care, improved access to care and reduced costs. Earlier in this book, the Triple Aim framework, as developed by the Institute for Healthcare Improvement (IHI, n.d.), was discussed in light of the key role that information technology plays in achieving the ultimate goal of the Triple Aim (i.e. performance improvement in healthcare). Achievement of the all of the elements of the Triple Aim Framework is dependent on the availability of electronic information (Jarrett, 2016). In the U.S. environment, many areas of health reform can be furthered and strengthened by focusing on the Triple Aim and by the implementation and integration of information technology.

"By providing greater insight to patients, providers, and policy makers into the appropriate application of interventions, and quality and costs of care, these data offer the opportunity to accelerate progress on the six dimensions of quality care" (as defined by the AHRQ—"safe, effective, patient-centered, timely, efficient, and equitable") (AHRQ, 2016).

The information that electronic systems can generate provides a high level of system performance value not otherwise attainable in healthcare. This type of value focuses on improved data capture, data sharing, reporting, use of evidence-based medicine, and improved communication by and between physicians, staff and patients. Electronic, secure data provides value such as: improved privacy and security, data sharing, data reporting, enhanced communication.

HIMSS, 2017

In the HIMSS Value STEPS™ Framework, the domain of Electronic Secure Data/Information is further detailed in three sub-domains:

■ Secure data/information
■ Communications
■ Data sharing and reporting

Sub-Domain: Securing Information and Infrastructure

A significant proportion of healthcare stakeholders have embraced the digital health revolution. PACS systems, hospital scheduling systems, laboratory systems, websites, EHRs, and health information exchange are just a few types of systems that create, maintain, transmit, and/or receive electronic information. Securing electronic information is a complex endeavor, especially since many of our information systems have to communicate with each other. Some of these information systems, too, may have legacy operating systems (e.g. DOS, Windows XP and others) and/or use legacy applications. Additionally, many systems are exposed to the Internet (i.e. external facing). Thus, search engines such as Shodan (www.shodan.io) or Censys (https://censys.io) may be used as tools to discover exposed endpoints, anonymous FTP servers and more. Many researchers and ethical hackers use resources such as these for good purposes. However, tools which are meant for good may also be used for malicious purposes (by those with malicious intent).

To stay ahead of threats, many healthcare organizations conduct regular risk assessments and penetration tests. According to the results of the 2018 HIMSS Cybersecurity Survey, 69.7% of respondents indicated that their healthcare organization conducts risk assessments at least once a year, while

57.1% claim their organization conducts penetration tests at least annually (HIMSS Cybersecurity Survey, 2018).

Hackers are not the only types of actors threatening healthcare organizations. According to the same 2018 HIMSS Cybersecurity Survey, online scam artists (e.g. phishing, spear phishing) and negligent insiders are the primary types of threat actors challenging healthcare organizations. To combat these threats, healthcare organizations use both "technical controls" and "human controls" to help reduce cyber risk (Barnum, Gegick and Michael, 2015).

While patients universally want their data to be private and secure, they seem to be receptive to the idea of sharing their personal data when it is de-identified and used for clinical research. In a study of 800 Californians, researchers reported in the *Journal of the American Medical Informatics Association*, that "consumers are in favor of electronic data sharing but elements of transparency are important: individual control, who has access and the purpose for use. Respondents were more likely to agree to share de-identified information for research than to share identified information for healthcare" (Kim et al., 2015). De-identified health information is important for the advancement of medicine and for the availability of evidence-base medicine as well as for the management of the health of populations. Yet, as the Institute of Medicine Roundtable on Value and Science Driven Health Care rightly points out, the challenge is that "few places, however, have comprehensive, longitudinal views about individuals. The inability to connect data that may include risk factors, medical history, and interventions in a comprehensive way is a fundamental flaw in moving forward" (Institute of Medicine Roundtable on Value and Science Driven Health Care, 2010).

Sub-Domain: Enhanced Communication

Communication between physicians and staff in the care of patients is critical in order to achieve care coordination and quality improvement; to reduce inaccurate information sharing; and to reduce waste and redundancy in care (e.g. duplicate testing). The EHR facilitates that communication by providing immediate access to the patient's clinical information in a secure environment without the geographical restraint of paper record locations (offices, desks in physicians' homes for evening work).

One of the critical areas or times in which access to complete and current information is important is during and immediately after transitions in care. Typically, transitions are those times in which patients are transferred between different units or services within a provider organization or from acute care to home or to another provider of services (e.g. rehabilitation facilities, nursing home). Transitions also happen within provider organizations when, for example, there is a shift change among staff or the patient is moved from one unit of care to another (e.g. ED to surgery to ICU). In each of these instances, a new team of clinicians and support staff assumes the care of the patient. The recent comprehensive history of the patient and his/her ongoing clinical care are critical information for the new caregivers. The case is strong for a focus on improved information transfer to achieve high-quality care coordination during transitions. However,

> one of the major barriers to coordinated and effective care transitions is poor communication between providers. Improving provider-to-provider communication can improve care transitions and reduce readmissions. Health information technology (IT), such as electronic health record (EHR) systems, can facilitate transitions in patient care by improving provider communication.

AHRQ, 2012

At the start of this chapter, systems theory was discussed. Systems theory offers insight into how to effectively bring together many, often disparate, parties or sub-units to achieve a high performance organization. One of the key structures for high performance in such organizations is communication. In healthcare, communication between and among physicians, staff, and patients is critical. The EHR, when fully used, has proven over and over again that it can help facilitate improved communication in this environment. Communication is enhanced in that it can happen more readily than in a paper-based environment; it can occur in real-time; and it can be complete. The caregivers can see the full record on the patient, and can be alerted immediately to urgent needs. Their ability to impact care is not reliant on their geographic location because with mobile devices they can access records, get alerts and up to date data in real-time. They can intervene early when there is a clinical crisis rather than experiencing the delay of waiting to get a paper record.

The EHR also supports communication through telemedicine bringing the expertise of highly specialized practitioners to distant locations and to patients who would otherwise not have access to medical advancements and services they need. For example, an EHR mobile app allows patients to securely connect to their records/data from any mobile device. This scenario plays out for patients throughout the country.

Sub-Domain: Data Sharing and Reporting

Electronic data collection has been made possible with the advent of the widespread adoption of EHRs. That wealth of data is a powerful asset, but it is at its richest if it is aggregated across the healthcare system and among the providers of care in a region, throughout the state and ultimately the country and globally. To achieve the value that this powerhouse represents means that all those who are involved with that data must be willing to share the data: patients, providers and payers. Glenn Steele, MD, phrases this cogently when he writes that:

> In order to harness the true potential and power of data and data sharing, providers, payers, and purchasers must be willing to work together to share cost and quality data across the entire health care system – it is no longer acceptable for providers, payers, and purchasers to treat data as a proprietary asset. Patients routinely transition from one provider to another, receiving care and services from different providers, health systems, and health plans. In too many instances, health data does not follow the patient, creating gaps in coverage and leading to fragmented, uncoordinated care that diminishes quality and drives up costs.

> **Steele, 2016**

When data does not follow the patient, the effect of this fosters the endurance of a fragmented system, uncoordinated care, high costs and lower quality. It also impedes clinical research and effectiveness in medical training.

Dr. David Sackett (one of the "fathers of EBM") and his colleagues define EBM as "a systematic approach to clinical problem solving which allows the integration of the best available research evidence with clinical expertise and patient values" (Sacket et al., 2000). Data provides the primary input (i.e. the substance, for EBM). As data and information are becoming easier to collect and analyze, the potential is increasing exponentially for developing improved access to evidence-based decision-making at the bedside, for achieving new advances in medicine and for improving the health of entire populations.

According to a report from Stanford University, some estimates suggest that the volume of clinical data is expanding by 48% annually.

The sheer volume of health care data is growing at an astronomical rate: 153 exabytes (one exabyte=one billion gigabytes) were produced in 2013 and an estimated 2,314 exabytes will be produced in 2020, translating to an overall rate of increase at least 48 percent annually.

Stanford Medicine, 2017

The opportunity to collect and maintain this data is in information technology and the ability to perform analysis of it through the continuing development of data science is expanding. Yet it faces continuing issues related to the need for technological development of more deeply and widely integrated information technology and to the cultural and strategic readiness of providers, payers and patients to share data.

According to a report published by RAND in 2017, overcoming some of the challenges to improved value capture in healthcare can further the availability and use of EBM by supporting, for example:

- New types of research and innovation associated with access to wider scale, more diverse and more stratified data;
- Operational efficiencies in clinical trials due to more precise recruitment, retention and site-selection strategies;
- Improved drug safety through more complete drug safety profiles over time and more comprehensive assessments of possible adverse events;
- Enhanced, data-enabled public health prevention and promotion as a result of more comprehensive data on risk factors, from a wide range of sources;
- Improved quality of healthcare (e.g. better diagnostic capabilities and more personalized clinical decision-making) as a result of improved markers, screening algorithms and predicative analytics; and
- Efficiency gains in care delivery through new prospects for data-enabled self-care and remote-care, when circumstances are appropriate (Ghiga et al., 2017).

Summary

In the function of organizational systems, data is an empowering force for improvement. It informs strategic decision-making and serves as the substantive focus of communication at all levels. Communication is essential for organizational systems to function, and this is particularly so for healthcare organizations.

Healthcare is in a transformational process. This process is evident in the trends toward a population focus and value-based care. Patients are viewed as being at the center of care, the relationship between practitioners and patients is changing and technology is evolving to further empower patients toward being proactive in their health and healthcare. All of this, and more, are evident in the growing demands for performance improvement, particularly in the clinical delivery of care. The re-shaping of healthcare is made possible because of the growing depth and breadth of data that is emerging through the use of the EHR. As was so cogently stated in the Stanford 2017 report: "Behind these trends is one fundamental force driving health care transformation: the power of data" (Stanford Medicine, 2017).

The value of the EHR as the foundational tool to make change possible is confirmed in the way in which it enables the collection, aggregation and analysis of health data from a wide array of sources. Long held principles of systems theory call for the unification and organization of disparate sub-units in an organization, all of which combine to make the organization as unified and effective whole. Healthcare organizations and their complexity have the opportunity for greater operational and clinical performance improvement with the availability of real-time and in-depth data for decision-making.

Discussion Questions

1. What is systems theory and what is the relationship of digital technology in the application of systems theory in healthcare?
2. How is the availability of the EHR of benefit to the patient?
3. What entities have an interest in healthcare data and how does the EHR help to meet their needs?
4. How does digital technology assist in ensuring the security of patient information?

CASE FOR DISCUSSION: UT SOUTHWESTERN MEDICAL CENTER

The story of UTSW is one of tremendous growth and progress. As early adopters of healthcare technology, UT Southwestern has embraced the benefits that automation and data analytics bring to clinical medicine, always keeping their goal of improved patient outcomes front-of-mind.

Access to vast amounts of clean interoperable data enables fast and reliable data-driven decision-making for UTSW. This framework allows data interoperability across multiple systems throughout the enterprise. The data is easily digested using Microsoft Power BI dashboards or other analytic tools. Through conformed dimensions and multiple fact tables, users can easily analyze data for immediate answers. This framework will allow UTSW to save approximately $2 million dollars annually.

Source: HIMSS, 2018: UT Southwestern: Davies Enterprise Award.

DISCUSSION QUESTIONS

In this brief case, UTSW describes the advanced use of data analytics to improve clinical outcomes. How did their digital technology support the organization in working toward their goal? What are the data characteristics that are important to improved medical decision-making? How does the improved automation drive monetary savings?

References

AHRQ. The six domains of Health Care Quality. 2016. https://www.ahrq.gov/professionals/quality-patient-safety/talkingquality/create/sixdomains.html. Accessed August 2, 2018.

Barnum S, Gegick M, and Michael, CC. Defense in depth: Maturity levels and audience indicators. September 5, 2015. www.us-cert.gov/bsi/articles/knowledge/principles/defense-in-depth. Accessed April 9, 2018.

Fisher C. Organisation development: Five core theories – systems theory – organization development. 2012. www.organisationdevelopment.org/five-core-theories-systems-theory-organisation-development/. Accessed March 5, 2018.

Ghiga I, Yang M and Knack AI. RAND study: Exploring the value of health data. April 27, 2017. www.rand.org/randeurope/research/projects/value-of-health-data.html. Accessed March 8, 2018.

HIMSS. Workflow considerations for C-CDA document exchange. November 7, 2017. www.himss.org/library/workflow-considerations-c-cda-document-exchange

HIMSS. UT Southwestern: Davies Enterprise Award. 2018. https://www.himss.org/library/ut-southwestern-davies-enterprise-award. Accessed April 20, 2018.

HIMSS Cybersecurity Survey. 2018. www.himss.org/sites/himssorg/files/u132196/2018_HIMSS_Cybersecurity_ Survey_Final_Report.pdf. Accessed April 9, 2018.

IHI. Triple Aim. n.d. www.ihi.org/Engage/Initiatives/TripleAim/Pages/default.aspx. Accessed March 7, 2018.

Institute of Medicine Roundtable on Value and Science Driven Health Care. Clinical data as the basic staple of health learning: Creating and Protecting a public good: Workshop summary (U.S. healthcare data today: Current state of play). 2010. www.ncbi.nlm.nih.gov/books/NBK54296/ Accessed March 8, 2018.

Jarrett, M. Fulfilling the promise of electronic health records. April 3, 2016. http://www.ihi.org/communities/blogs/_layouts/15/ihi/community/blog/itemview.aspx?List=7d1126ec-8f63-4a3b-9926-c44ea3036813&ID=231. Accessed August 3, 2018.

Katz and Khan. Systems theory (images explaining the theory). 1966–1967. https://images.search.yahoo.com/yhs/search?p=Kataz+and+Khan+systems+theory&fr=yhs-iry-fullyhosted_011&hspart=iry&hsimp=yhs-fullyhosted_011&imgurl=http%3A%2F%2Fimage.slidesharecdn.com%2F01orgnlchangemodels-130127233550-phpapp01%2F95%2Forganizational-change-models-10-638.jpg%3Fcb%3D1369368859#id=80&iurl=http%3A%2F%2Fslideplayer.com%2F9363745%2F28%2Fimages%2F48%2FCommunicating%2Bfor%2BResults%252C%2B10th%2Bedition.jpg&action=click. Accessed March 5, 2018.

Kelvin, Lord (Sir William Thomson) quotations. 1883. https://zapatopi.net/kelvin/quotes/. Accessed March 1, 2018.

Kim KK, Joseph JG and Ohno-Machado L. Comparison of consumers' views on electronic data sharing for healthcare research. *Journal of the American Medical Informatics Association*, vol. 22, no. 4. March 31, 2015. https://academic.oup.com/jamia/article/22/4/821/1746283. Accessed March 8, 2018.

New York University School of Medicine. Definition taken from *BMJ* 1996; 312:71–72. https://library.med.nyu.edu/library/instruction/handouts/pdf/ebmdefinitions.pdf. Accessed March 20, 2018.

NTOCC. Transition of care measures. 2008. www.ntocc.org/Portals/0/PDF/Resources/TransitionsOfCare_Measures.pdf. Accessed March 15, 2018.

Sackett DL, Strauss SE, Richardson WS et al. *Evidence-Based Medicine: How to Practice and Teach EBM*. 2000. London: Churchill-Livingstone.

Stanford Medicine. Health trends report: Harnessing the power of data in health. June 2017. https://med.stanford.edu/content/dam/sm/sm-news/documents/StanfordMedicineHealthTrendsWhitePaper2017.pdf

Steele G, The culture of data sharing has to change. *Health Affairs*. September 20, 2016. www.healthaffairs.org/do/10.1377/hblog20160920.056663/full/. Accessed March 8, 2018.

University of Michigan Medical School. Office of Research: De-identified data sets. 2016. https://research.medicine.umich.edu/office-research/institutional-review-boards-irbmed/privacy-board/de-identified-data-sets. Accessed March 12, 2018.

Chapter 6

Patient Engagement and Population Management

Kendall Cortelyou-Ward and Kathryn Thompson

Learning Objectives

- Describe the importance of population health management.
- Identify the role of information technology in population health management.
- Articulate the value of activated and engaged patients.
- Describe how health information technology can improve patient engagement.

Definitions

- *Population health*: The health outcomes of a group of individuals, including the distribution of such outcomes within the group.
- *Patient engagement*: A concept and strategy that involves the tools and actions taken by patients to manage their own health.

Introduction

This chapter addresses two key strategies (or sub-domains in the vernacular of the HIMSS Value STEPS™ Framework) in the national effort to improve value delivered by healthcare institutions in return for the commitment of funding and other resources that is made to them. The two key strategies are:

1. *Improvement in population health*: As defined above, population health relates to the health of groups of individuals. In order to achieve improvement, information is needed about the population's aggregate status, which transcends the health status of one individual, but must address each of the individuals in the group. For example, if lowering the rate of diabetes in the population is a specific population health goal, then it is important to improve the diabetic health of as many individuals in the group as possible. Both individual and aggregate measures of performance must be targeted.

2. *Improvement in patient engagement*: In the current environment, population health measures and goals are focused primarily on chronic and preventable conditions. In each of these, patient engagement is a key part of achieving improvement. Patients must be informed and willing to actively participate in their care, e.g. to take their medicines, get screenings when scheduled, and actively comply with diet and exercise routines.

Sub-Domain: Improvement in Population Health

The concept of population health has gained a lot of attention in recent years and refers to "the health outcomes of a group of individuals, including the distribution of such outcomes within the group" (Kindig and Stoddart, 2003). Often these populations are defined by geographic region. However, rather than just countries or states, a population can also be other defined groups such as ethnic groups, university students, the elderly, employees or those with certain health conditions such as diabetes.

Population health is made up of three distinct components: health outcomes, health determinants and policies that prompt interventions. Social determinants of health (SDOH) include healthcare access, individual behavior, environment and genetics. SDOH directly affect health outcomes and vice-versa. Furthermore, health outcomes are sub-divided into two components—means and disparities. Means of health outcomes, such as age at death or quality of life, are often directly related and impacted by disparities in race or ethnicity, socioeconomic status, geographic location and gender.

Within an organization or health system, population health is often addressed by utilizing population health management (PHM) approaches, concepts and programs. PHM can be best defined as a process that uses "big data" and the derived analytics to describe specific populations, assess risks, deliver targeted care and report on the health outcomes. The discipline of PHM aggregates patient data and information across a plethora of HIT platforms and interfaces. More importantly, PHM provides the actions in which providers can improve an organization's clinical and financial outcomes. Simply put, the goal of PHM is to improve the health of a group of individuals at the lowest possible cost.

What Drives Costs?

The United States spends more on healthcare than any other developed nation and many factors, not just one, contribute to the increasing healthcare costs in the country. Compared to similar established nations, the United States devotes nearly 20% of gross domestic product on healthcare spending. Past and current research supports that improving population health initiatives will have a direct impact on the rising costs. In order to achieve this goal of financial control, it is essential to focus on key components on which population health and PHM have direct effect. Key areas of cost reduction include focusing on preventative care, decreasing readmission rates, and reducing emergency room utilization. This also includes a significant emphasis on the management of chronic diseases, immunizations, screenings and patient education.

Why Is Population Health Important?

Population health is important because it focuses on the health of everyday individuals and the groups to which they belong. The main priority of population health is to reduce health inequities and health disparities among the different population groups that exist. These inequities can be due to many SDOH incorporating all factors that populations are born into, live and work in. SDOH includes social, environmental, cultural and physical factors and affect how individuals function, their quality of life, their health outcomes and risks.

Moreover, population health can help reduce the frequency of health emergencies and costly healthcare episodes associated with emergency department visits and inpatient stays. Economically, an investment in population health programs and efficient PHM tools can positively affect outcomes within a community or area.

What Is the Role of Information Technology in Population Health?

In the current health environment, providers and various payers continue to develop, evaluate and adopt new ways to manage population health. Often, these new strategies leverage the advancement in information technology to achieve the wanted scale, quality and efficiency needed to affect population health in significant areas. HIT has the ability to revolutionize the way that population health is managed and provides tools for providers, patients and researchers (Dowding, 2016).

HIT offers new, more efficient ways for providers to monitor, intervene and interact with their patients. HIT involves the collection of patient data from a variety of sources, analysis of patient data, the assessment of risk and evidence for action in order to improve health and financial outcomes. With respect to the patient, HIT provides additional resources for patients to better manage and participate in their own healthcare. If executed properly, HIT increases the likelihood for PHM programs and strategies to promote overall better health and reduces the need for costly interventions (Diamond, Mostashari and Shirky 2009).

HIT Tools to Support Population Health

- EHRs and patient registries:

    Data-driven PHM tools are essential in advancing information technology for improved population health. EHR and patient registries help providers identify patients, patient risk factors, earmark interventions for individuals or communities, access and manage key patient data and establish continuity of care. With the availability of patient information through EHRs and registries, providers and organizations are able to respond to existing and developing gaps in quality of care.

    EHRs represent a single patient record that is a comprehensive collection of clinical and administrative data. Registries are collections of information about a group of patients who share similar medical conditions or who have had similar experiences. On the patient level, both EHRs and patient registries use clinical information; however, registries in particular are population focused. They are frequently defined by a disease or exposure and are designed to provide outcome projections before information can be fully collected and assessed (Gliklich et al., 2014). By interfacing both platforms, it allows data and patient information to concentrate in one area, data visualization is optimized, metrics are highlighted and decision-making surrounding population health is streamlined.

■ Health information exchange

Patient data is often constructed using diverse medical terminology and stored in multiple formats; adding to the complexity and costly nature of the digital process. Recent healthcare legislation and actions support the adoption of Health information exchanges (HIE) in order to correct the fragmentation of patient health information (Vest and Gamm, 2010). HIEs are HIT tools that allow secure sharing of clinical information with numerous providers and the patient. HIEs have been shown to increase healthcare efficiency, quality of care and healthcare reporting, and improve communication of clinical information between all stakeholders (Shapiro et al., 2011). Key stakeholders that benefit from the exchange of personal information in HIEs other than the patient and provider include physician organizations, health insurance plans and ACOs.

Currently, two types of HIEs exist: public and private. Public HIE, also referred to as community exchanges, are open to, supported by and facilitated by the communities in which they operate. Alternatively, private HIEs are managed by a single healthcare entity or integrated delivery network (Lento, 2013). Although both are effective models, private HIEs offer better data control and are often more cost effective.

■ Patient portals

As population health moves to the forefront, healthcare providers are increasingly recognizing that engaging patients is essential to providing quality, cost effective care. One way to achieve high levels of patient engagement is through the adoption of patient portals. Patient portals are secure access websites in which a patient can access their own personal health information. In addition to increasing the efficiency and productivity of health administration, patient portals can provide a platform for patients to participate in their own health decisions and provide customization for preventative care based on the individual patients' risk factors (Price-Haywood et al., 2017).

Particularly when combined with EHR, patient portals have the ability to improve quality of health and ease access to healthcare amenities. Portals can offer components such as provider centric messaging, provider alerts, timely access to labs and test results and access for family members or healthcare givers. Furthermore, patients have the increased potential to communicate with their health providers, access their own medical records, schedule follow-up appointments, access-billing information and manage prescription refills. All features of patient portals have the potential to increase responsiveness to patient needs, quality of care for the patient, affect chronic disease management and address population disparities.

■ Telehealth/telemedicine

Telecommunication technologies enable delivery of healthcare to patients located in rural and inaccessible locations. Telehealth and telemedicine are clear solutions to address the challenges of geographic location and scarcity of resources while simultaneously helping providers manage health outcomes. Telemedicine is defined as the provision of healthcare services, information and education over a long distance. Telehealth, which encompasses telemedicine, refers to the interaction or communication between patient and health provider (Maheu, Whitten and Allen 2002).

Telehealth equipment can be used to monitor health statistics such as blood pressure, pulse and temperature from a distance. Data collected can be used by physicians to gain a more accurate description of disease status over a prolonged period of time and also use that data to make better decisions regarding the patient's care. Telehealth can increase access to care by reducing travel time for patients, bridging gaps in healthcare by offering access to specialty providers and engaging patients through outreach and pre-office visit planning (Stowe and Harding, 2010). Goals also include the ability for patients to self-manage their own care, reduce admission rates and reduce costs in the long run.

Advanced Population Analytics

Analytic applications are used in HIT to better manage a population of patients by providing a single, integrated view of regulatory, performance and composite health measures. Analytic platforms have the capability to not only measure and benchmark performance, but also the applications have the ability to pinpoint statistical outliers and address issues that might drive up cost. Measures tracked and recorded by a healthcare organization can include reports and statistics for disease management, preventative care and medication management. Additional features of advanced population analytics include:

■ Stratifying patient populations according to disease type, treatment, risk and outcomes.
■ Monitor metrics in real-time and compare across national benchmarks.
■ Enact interventions from within the application that align with patient care plans.

Sub-Domain: Improved Patient Engagement

What Is an Engaged Patient? Why Is Patient Engagement Important?

Patient engagement is a concept and strategy that involves the tools and actions taken by patients to manage their own health. The strategy integrates the knowledge, ability and the willingness for that patient to participate in their own health decisions. Engaged patients are educated, enabled and proactive about their health. They regularly ask questions and communicate what they feel is important to their providers. Increasingly, communities and the patient's family also play a significant role.

The goals of patient engagement are to improve health outcomes, promote healthy behaviors and reduce the cost of health services overall. Increasingly, engagement is achieved using health self-management tools and services such as patient portals and HIEs. Through these HIT tools, patients are able to have access to their own medical records and lab tests, providing transparency and enabling them to make well informed choices.

Patient Activation Measure

Rather than being tied to specific patient behaviors, patient activation reflects the attitude and approach to self-management of one's own healthcare. Patient activation, or the level in which a patient is involved in their own healthcare, is a broad, general and quantifiable concept that is defined by the patient activation measure (PAM). PAM is a 100-point quantifiable scale consisting of 22 survey components organized under four categories of patient activation: (1) believing the patient role in activation is important, (2) having the confidence and knowledge necessary to take action, (3) actually taking action to maintain and improve one's health and (4) staying the course even under stress (Hibbard et al., 2004).

PAM is used to determine the activation level, or level of engagement for a patient before and after health interventions. Often, PAM can be used by providers and organizations to improve patient outcomes in the long run, reduce costs and evaluate patient engagement programs. Research shows that patients at a higher level of activation experience fewer episodes of emergency care and more often disengage in unhealthy behaviors, such as smoking and overeating (Hibbard et al., 2013). From a physician standpoint, high patient activation can help shape healthcare agendas and better explore options that are optimal for the patient.

How Health Information Technology Impacts Population Health and Patient Engagement— Results from the STEPS™ Database

Population Health

The HIMSS STEPS™ Database clearly shows the impact that HIT has on improving the health of the population. Specifically, improvements in prevention was cited over 500 times in cases reviewed by the HIMSS team.

Managing Chronic Conditions

As of 2012, about half of all adults in America had one or more chronic health conditions, and two of the most common chronic diseases, heart disease and cancer, accounted for nearly 46% of all deaths in 2014. As of 2015, 68% of adults over the age of 65 had at least two chronic conditions. Treating individuals with these conditions accounts for most of the U.S. healthcare costs (CDC.gov).

Increasingly, providers are using HIT to help patients manage these chronic conditions. The STEPS™ Database contains over 150 values statements related to improving the management of chronic conditions and offers examples of how EHRs, telehealth, and m-Health can improve control of blood pressure, diabetes, COPD, HIV and other illnesses. Control of hypertension is a consistent theme in the database, where case studies indicate that the EHR serves as a prompt to providers to follow-up on blood pressure, offers patient education materials and support medication adherence.

Preventative Care

Central to the mission of population health is a focus on preventative care and applying interventions when appropriate. The STEPS™ Database includes over 350 value statements related to improving preventative care, demonstrating the impact that HIT can have on the health of the population including decreasing obesity, increasing immunizations and screenings, improving smoking cessation and other general preventative care activities. Most notably, giving healthcare organizations the ability to analyze the patient population, identify high-risk patients and intervene with appropriate preventative care is a common theme.

Patient Engagement

Engaging patients using HIT is a common theme in the HIMSS STEPS™ Database, cited almost 800 times in the cases reviewed. Most often cited are improvements in patient education, patient engagement and use of the patient portal.

Patient Education

The importance of patient education and ensuring that patients have access to educational materials was brought to the forefront when the Meaningful Use 2 guidelines made patient-specific educational materials a core menu item. To meet the Meaningful Use objective providers must "use certified EHR technology to identify patient-specific resources and provide those resources to the patient." The STEPS™ Database captured 244 instances of health information technology improving patient education and improving the distribution of educational materials. Specifically, the ability of HIT enabled patient education materials allow the provider to customize for specific patient needs. Examples from STEPS™ Framework include interactive educational materials, including those that vary based of reading level and language.

Discussion Questions

1. Often, the definition of population health and public health are used interchangeably. However, the definitions and meanings are different. What is the main difference between population and public health?
2. Using your definitions from question 1, who are the drivers and stakeholders behind each: population health and public health? List examples of how the stakeholders accomplish population health initiatives and public health programs.
3. Populations and characteristics of populations vary across demographics and geographic regions. For each population, health and the definition

of health changes. What would be your definition of health that could apply to all populations?

4. What are some of the key determinants and factors that contribute to the increase or decrease in health for different populations?

5. Federal and state policies dictate what happens around health in the United States. What recent policies, enacted by either government, might affect population health in your area? Do these policies positively or negatively affect these populations?

CASES FOR DISCUSSION

CASE #6.1: KRESSLY PEDIATRICS

Dr. Kressly came to the Doylestown, PA area in 1990 and joined a local practice. After learning about the area, she created Kressly Pediatrics, a smaller, more personalized environment where she could really get to know her patients and families. As a start, her practice decided to expand the use of their EHR.

Kressly Pediatrics recognized the importance of closely adhering to the American Academy of Pediatrics "Recommendations for preventive pediatric healthcare," and decided to use them as a framework for maximizing patient outcomes through an internal initiative to improve wellness visit rates. In order to achieve this, the organization set internal goals to transition from reactive to proactive PHM internally.

Kressly realized that not all children in their practice were receiving wellness visits at the periodic times outlined for optimum care. Kressly leveraged existing core HIT functionality in their EHR to flag patients who were overdue for well visits. As a result, wellness visit rates rose from 66% in 2013 to 93% in 2016.

Source: HIMSS, 2017a: Kressly Pediatrics: Davies Ambulatory Award.

DISCUSSION QUESTIONS

The above short case describes how one doctor used her digital technology to improve the health of the population in her service area. What challenges do you think she might have had in doing this? When the practice transitioned from "reactive to proactive population management," what exactly were they doing? What tactics might a practice use to achieve this transition? How would digital health technologies help in the process? How would Dr. Kressly integrate or interact with public health agencies in her population health efforts?

CASE #6.2: NORTHERN OHIO MEDICAL SPECIALISTS

By improving quality metrics, Northern Ohio Medical Specialists (NOMS) Healthcare has observed a significant impact on health outcomes. In 2016, the organization's healthcare bacterial pneumonia hospital rate decreased to 6.46%, down from 14.62% in 2013. This rate is below all of ACO's and FFS's Medicare patients. As a result of these efforts, NOMS improved their pneumonia vaccination rates from 33% in 2013 to their current rate of 83%.

Source: HIMSS, 2017b: Northern Ohio Medical Specialists (NOMS): Davies Ambulatory Award.

DISCUSSION QUESTIONS

Northern Ohio Medical Specialists improved their health outcomes through the use of their EHR. These achievements occur through both the use of digital technologies and through human effort. Explain the human side of the improvements they achieved both in the hospital and outside the hospital (i.e. who was likely involved and what did they have to do to make the positive change?). With a bit of research, find out what the bacterial pneumonia hospital rate is among ACO and FFS's Medicare patients.

References

Caloyeras JP, Liu H, Exum E, Broderick M and Mattke S. Managing manifest diseases, but not health risks, saved PepsiCo money over seven years. *Health Affairs.* 2014; 33(1), 124–131.

Diamond CC, Mostashari F and Shirky C. Collecting and sharing data for population health: A new paradigm. *Health Affairs.* 2009; 28(2), 454–466. doi:10.1377/hlthaff.28.2.454.

Dowding M. The role of IT in population health management. www.hfma.org/Leadership/PopulationHealthIT/. Posted 2016. Accessed March 22, 2018.

Gliklich RE, Dreyer NA and Leavy MB. Interfacing registries with electronic health records. https://ahrq-ehc-application.s3.amazonaws.com/media/pdf/registries-ehr_research.pdf. Posted 2014. Accessed March 21, 2018.

Hibbard JH, Stockard J, Mahoney ER and Tusler M. Development of the Patient Activation Measure (PAM): Conceptualizing and measuring activation in patients and consumers. *Health Services Research.* 2004; 39(4 pt 1), 1005–1026.

Hibbard JH, Stockard J, Mahoney ER et al. Patient activation measure. *Behavioral Medicine.* 2013; 4, 391–396.

HIMSS. Kressly Pediatrics: Davies Ambulatory Award. 2017a. www.himss.org/library/kressly-pediatrics-daviesambulatory-award-0.

HIMSS. Northern Ohio Medical Specialists (NOMS): Davies Ambulatory Award. 2017b. www.himss.org/library/northern-ohio-medicalspecialists-noms-davies-ambulatory-award.

Kindig DA and Stoddart G. What is population health? *American Journal of Public Health.* 2003; 93, 366–369.

Lento J. The relationship between HIE and population health management. www.wellcentive.com/blog/the-relationship-between-hie-and-population-health-management/. Posted November 13, 2013. Accessed February 20, 2018.

Maheu M, Whitten P and Allen A. E-Health, telehealth and telemedicine: A guide to startup and success. John Wiley & Sons, New York. 2002.

Price-Haywood E G, Harden-Barrios J, Luo Q and Ulep R. eHealth Literacy: Patient engagement in identifying strategies to encourage use of patient portals among older adults. 2017; *Population Health Management,* 20(6), 486–494.

Shapiro JS, Mostashari F, Hripcsak G, Soulakis N and Kuperman G. Using health information exchange to improve public health. *American Journal of Public Health.* 2011; 101(4), 616–623. doi.org/10.2105/AJPH.2008.158980. Accessed March 23, 2018.

Stowe S and Harding S. Telecare, telehealth and telemedicine. *European Geriatric Medicine.* 2010; 1(3), 193–197.

Vest JR and Gamm LD. Health information exchange: Persistent challenges and new strategies. *Journal of the American Medical Informatics Association,* 2010; 17(3), 288–294.

Chapter 7

Savings

Lorren Pettit

Learning Objectives

- Explain why Savings is an important domain in the STEPS™ model.
- Identify at least one reason why there is a debate about the positive financial impact of HIT in healthcare organizations.
- Describe the sub-values of the Savings domain.

Definitions

- *Efficiency:* A level of performance that describes a process that uses the lowest amount of inputs to create the greatest amount of outputs (Investopedia, Efficiency, n.d.).
- *Operational efficiency:* Non-financial savings realized from the elimination of waste through HIT enhanced workflow processes.
- *Productivity:* An economic measure of output per unit of input (Investopedia, Productivity, n.d.).
- *Return on investment (ROI):* A calculation used to determine whether a proposed investment is wise and how well it will repay the investor. It is calculated as the ratio of the amount gained (taken as positive) or lost (taken as negative), relative to the basis.

Foundational Elements

The fifth and final STEPS™ domain, Savings, is the domain many leaders tend to first mention when discussing the benefits of HIT. Understandable, as this domain directly addresses the financial impact of HIT.

Admittedly, HIT implementation is an expensive endeavor for any healthcare organization, as it involves a number of upfront (e.g. physical hardware and/or software, staff expenses for setup, training, etc.) and ongoing expenses (e.g. IT support, system updates, etc.). For many organizations, especially smaller medical practices or nursing homes with lower cash flow, cost alone prohibits the ability to properly implement and maintain a HIT system. Layered on top of the expense of the system, is a priority placed on financial performance in the healthcare sector. For example, "financial improvement challenges" once again topped the list of CEO concerns in the 2016 American College of Healthcare Executives' annual survey of top issues confronting hospital. (American College of Healthcare Executives, 2017). Given the aforementioned factors, the inherent interest in demonstrated financial benefits associated with savings is not surprising.

Addressing the financial impacts of HIT is an area within which CIOs must be comfortable, especially if the CIO desires to be aligned with the strategic priorities of his/her C-suite peers. IT leaders are key players in the cost improvement conversation through their stewardship of organization-wide IT expenditures and enabling cost savings initiatives to produce real savings.

Yet championing the benefit of HIT can be a losing argument if defined solely in terms of financial measures. Despite the financial savings promise of HIT, demonstrating the financial impact of HIT has not been a "slam dunk" exercise. Indeed, there has long been a debate about HIT's financial effects, both on individual providers and payers at the microeconomic level and on the U.S. healthcare system at the macroeconomic level (Sidorov, 2006; Congressional Budget Office, 2008). Much of this debate stems from the complicated nature of accounting for the financial impact of HIT. There are a myriad of intervening variables that need to be taken into consideration when assessing the causation linkage between a technological intervention and financial performance (e.g. user proficiency with the technology; etc.). This may explain in part why there is a limited number of articles on this topic, especially ones with strong study designs and financial analyses (Chaudhry et al., 2006; Goldzweig et al., 2009).

Another explanation as to why debates swirl around the financial benefits of HIT concerns the time horizon over which financial impacts are measured. Understandably, healthcare leaders are looking to realize the promise that HIT can deliver as soon as possible. Yet evidence suggests there is a lag time before organizations are in a position to benefit financially from their HIT investments. For example, researchers in one study found that HIT is initially associated with a 25%–33% decline in worker productivity during the initial implementation phases of the EMR (Bhargava and Mishra, 2014). As these declines translate into financial performance in a multiplicity of ways, it is not unreasonable to conclude financial assessments of HIT conducted shortly after the system is implemented, are less than impressive.

Despite the challenges in demonstrating the financial savings gained from HIT, it is not a conversation HIT leaders need to shun. Evidence does exist that HIT yields clear financial and operational savings for healthcare organizations. Accordingly, the HIMSS Value STEPS™ Savings domain is composed of the following two sub-domains;

- Non-financial measures (Operational efficiencies) and
- Financial measures (Cost savings)

Operational Efficiency

The operational efficiency refers to resource (e.g. time saved) savings realized from the elimination of waste through HIT enhanced workflow processes. The savings directly measured in this sub-domain are not discussed in financial terms, but are critical measures nonetheless in the calculation of the financial impact of HIT.

To fully appreciate the concept of *Savings* as used in the context of operational efficiency it is essential to clearly differentiate the terms *productivity* and *efficiency*. While these words tend to be used interchangeably in modern discourse, there is a notable technical difference. Productivity is an economic measure of output per unit of input (Investopedia, Productivity, n.d.). Inputs typically include labor and capital, while output measures vary by the item produced. Outputs in healthcare delivery are most often discussed in terms of revenues but can include clinical quality measures. Productivity is a non-comparative measure, meaning the measure exclusively refers to a singular input-output operational process.

Efficiency on the other hand involves the comparison of multiple input-output operational processes (productions). Efficiency only occurs when one operational process is compared to another operational process and one of the following conditions exist:

■ one is found to use proportionately fewer inputs to create the same proportionate number of outputs;
■ one is found to use proportionately the same number of inputs but creates proportionately more outputs;
■ both use the same proportionate number of inputs to create the same proportionate number of outputs.

The technical term used to refer to the difference between an efficient operational process and a less efficient process, is *waste*. It is the imperative of operational leaders in any organization to ensure their operations are as efficient as possible by eliminating identifiable waste in work processes. The *Savings* realized from operational efficiencies reflects the avoidance of non-financial and financial operational waste through HIT enhanced work processes.

With this understanding, there are a myriad of instances where HIT systems can eliminate non-financial operational waste. This is perhaps most easily evidenced in the use of voice-recognition systems to replace transcription services.

CASE #7.1: CHILDREN'S NATIONAL HEALTH SYSTEM

To illustrate, one health system in the mid-Atlantic region of the U.S. documented its operational efficiency savings in a HIMSS Davies Award submission (Children's National Health System). As a large specialty hospital processing approximately 250,000 transcriptions annually, hospital leaders recognized several concerns related to their paper-based clinical documentation process:

■ Dictated specialist notes were not available to view for 24 hours or more raising significant patient safety concerns.
■ Transcription process averaged 10 hours.
■ Once available, there was limited access to medical records for providers and families.
■ Transcription costs exceeded $1.6 million annually.

These findings led the leaders to conclude their workflow was inefficient, costly and a barrier to optimal care.

To address these concerns, the organization elected to implement an ambulatory EHR and voice-recognition system for the 450 Clinical Specialists working in their clinics. The solution they settled on immediately affected the efficiency of the workflow process as the number of steps to produce a clinical note reduced from 19 steps to 6 steps. Operational efficiency was also released when analyzing the organization's average transcription processing time. Over a two-year period, the organization reduced transcription volume by 93.4%, resulting in the average transcription processing time reduced by 100% (from 10.4 hours to 0 hours).

Source: HIMSS, 2017: Children's National Health System: Davies Enterprise Award.

Cost Savings

The use of HIT has long been championed as having tremendous potential to improve the operational efficiency and cost-effectiveness of healthcare systems. The realization of these benefits is especially important in the context of continued increases in healthcare costs and pervasive waste due to inefficient processes. When used effectively, HIT can enable providers to realize financial savings as a result of operational efficiencies. As operational activities are always associated with some type of operational expense, the reduction of operational waste should naturally be equated with some type of financial savings. Evidence in one study found that healthcare organizations most commonly experienced cost savings in pharmaceuticals and general acute or emergent care costs (Low et al., 2013).

Leveraging the case study detailed in the previous section helps demonstrate the association between operational efficiencies and cost savings. By using a voice-recognition system to reduce the annual volume of clinical notes requiring transcription from 250,000 to 19,000 notes over a two-year period, the organization reducing its annual transcription expense from over $1.6 million to $105,000. This represents a 93.4% reduction in transcription processing time and the avoidance of approximately $1.6 million in expenses (cost savings).

Return on Investment (ROI)

Frequently discussions around the cost savings of digital health technologies ultimately land on the discussion of ROI. ROI is a common business metric used to quantify the benefit (or loss) an investor receives in relation to a particular investment cost. Often expressed as net return (e.g. income) divided by the original cost of the investment, the higher the ROI ratio, the greater the benefit earned. ROI is one of the most used profitability ratios because of the array of financial variables that can be included in the calculus. That said, a significant downside of the ROI calculation is that it is an exclusively financial measure. As such, ROI calculations fail to describe the intangible benefits of an intervention. Whereas in other sectors there is a clear causal linkage between investment costs and income derived from the use of the technology, it is arguably a much more complicated calculus in healthcare. In digital health, the measures of return can be disguised in ambiguous qualitative health outcome terms like "patient activation," "behavior change" and "value-based pricing." Understandable, as qualitative and health outcome improvements are core to the healthcare provider's business.

Leaders therefore need to address what role these technology "ripple-effect" factors could/should play in an ROI calculation. If they do attempt to bring qualitative and health outcomes into the ROI formula, they are then challenged to take a multidimensional concept like health outcomes, quantify it into a metric and then somehow attribute fiscal value to the "resulting variable." This approach is obviously fraught with challenges as there may be little consensus in what dimensions to include in a measure and what fiscal value can be assigned to the measure of interest. While there are a myriad of ROI models allowing investors to select an approach that best suits their goals, the variability in models presents a challenge for those whose ROI goals vary from the audiences to whom they are presenting. When using ROI to compare investments, it is important to use the same inputs to get an accurate comparison.

Despite the challenges to ROI calculations, there is still an appetite (need) for health leaders to use financial measures to quantify the return benefit from their HIT investments. The demand for ROI calculations has accelerated with the shift to value-based care, as providers need even more metrics to support system-wide efforts to improve quality, lower costs and enhance the patient experience. While there is no one universally agreed upon approach for quantifying digital health returns, models surrounding investment expenses do exist. Models, like those offered through organizations like HIMSS, provide an array of investment and expense categories that HIT leaders can use as a basis to guide the creation of their own ROI profile.

EXHIBIT #7.1: HIMSS IT ROI MODEL

Presented as an Excel document, the HIMSS IT ROI Model provides users with an array of costs typically associated with HIT acquisition/implementation. Grouped into four major expense categories, the spreadsheet allows users to add, subtract and modify specific expenses as deemed appropriate to their particular situation. The following reflect the various "hard costs" included in the HIMSS ROI calculator:

■ Implementation capital
  – *Software licenses*
  – *Hardware*

■ Development
  – *Labor—internal*
  – *Labor—consultants*
  – *Labor—travel*

■ Implementation expenses
  – *Labor—internal*
  – *Labor—consultants*
  – *Change management*
  – *Training—IT*
  – *Training—users*
  – *Travel*
  – *Miscellaneous*
  – *Vendor training*

■ Annual reoccurring costs
  – *Labor—new positions*
  – *Software maintenance*
  – *Server maintenance*
  – *Administration/support*

Source: HIMSS, 2007: Template for HIMSS IT ROI model.

Determining ROI for HIT systems is a daunting task for any organization. Many of the investments dedicated to the system as well as the benefits derived from these technologies are notoriously difficult to measure. The measures included in the HIMSS IT ROI model above provide a basis from which organizations can start their ROI calculation journey. In general, casting a broader net to encompass both hard dollar and soft metrics, such as care coordination and quality, will allow an organization to achieve a more complete ROI measurement that best meets its needs.

Summary

The STEPS™ Savings domain is a critical domain of the model as the evidence in this area considers the financial impact of HIT. The Savings domain does not exclusively deal with financial measures though as the sub-domains bifurcate in direct financial saving evidence (cost savings) and indirect savings (operational efficiencies). Cost savings are most often preceded by operational efficiencies.

References

American College of Healthcare Executives. Survey: Healthcare finance, safety and quality cited by CEOs as top issues confronting hospitals in 2016. January 31, 2017. https://www.ache.org/pubs/Releases/2017/top-issues-confronting-hospitals-2016.cfm. Accessed March 22, 2018.

Bhargava HK, Mishra AN. Electronic medical records and physician productivity: Evidence from panel data analysis. *Management Science*. 2014; 60(10): 2543–2562.

Chaudhry B, Wang J, Wu S et al. Systemic review: Impact of health information technology on quality, efficiency, and costs of medical care. *Annuals of Internal Medicine*. 2006; 144(10): 742–752.

Congressional Budget Office. Evidence on the costs and benefits of health information technology: A CBO paper. 2008. Washington, DC.

Goldzweig CL, Towfigh A, Maglione M and Shekelle PG. Costs and benefits of health information technology: New trends from the literature. *Health Affairs*. 2009; 28(2): 282–293.

HIMSS. Template for HIMSS IT ROI model (Excel document). www.himss.org/template-himss-it-roi-model-excel-document. 2007. Accessed March 22, 2018.

HIMSS. Children's National Health System: Davies Enterprise Award. 2017. www.himss.org/sites/himssorg/files/improve-documentation-ehr-childrens-national.pdf. Accessed March 22, 2018.

Investopedia. Terms – Efficiency. n.d. www.investopedia.com/terms/e/efficiency.asp. Accessed March 22, 2018.

Investopedia. Terms – Productivity. n.d. www.investopedia.com/terms/p/productivity.asp. Accessed March 22, 2018.

Low AF, Phillips AB, Ancker JS et al. Financial effects of health information technology: A systemic review. *The American Journal of Managed Care*. 2013: 19(10); SP369–SP376.

Sidorov J. It ain't necessarily so: the electronic health record and the unlikely prospect of reducing health care costs. *Health Affairs*. 2006; 25(4): 1079–1085.

Chapter 8

Inter-Relationships of the Domains in the STEPS™ Value Framework

Lorren Pettit

Introduction

Up to this point in time, the presentation of the STEPS™ domains in this textbook suggest the benefits of HIT are fairly easy to catalogue. This simplistic treatment of the subject is understandable given the introductory purpose of the previous chapters. Yet there is a complexity to the categorization of beneficial evidence in the STEPS™ Framework that should be acknowledged. This chapter explores the challenges of the model and considerations users should have when using the framework to articulate the value of HIT.

Learning Objectives

- Identify the potential challenges IT professionals may encounter when leveraging the STEPS™ model to catalogue the benefits of HIT.
- Explain the difference between a health IT feature and a HIT benefit.
- Demonstrate how to use the feature-benefit matrix to associate HIT benefits with a HIT feature.

■ Detail how evidence in the "T," "E" and "P" domains of the STEPS™ Framework more directly reflect the causal linkages between HIT interventions and outcomes, than the evidence included in the Satisfaction and Savings domains.

Features and Benefits

Perhaps one of the most significant challenges in using the STEPS™ Framework is to differentiate "HIT features" from "HIT benefits." While the two concepts are related, the distinction is critical in ensuring the use of the appropriate evidence to advance the value narrative of HIT. Unfortunately, the distinction between the two ideas is often blurred and people are unsuccessful in their attempts to articulate the value of a HIT initiative when using features as evidence for value.

The "feature versus benefit" problem is not unique to HIT. This situation is a common issue many marketing professionals encounter when working with a product. Before addressing why people sometimes substitute HIT features for HIT benefits, it is essential to establish the difference between these terms.

Product/health IT features refer to functional characteristics of a product. When focusing on a product feature, marketers highlight something the product has or is, albeit a fundamental function of the product or the product's "shiny bells and whistles." In the consumer-world, product features include such things as razors with five-blade heads, power drills with interchangeable bits, or refrigerators that make crushed ice. In HIT, product features reflect things such as a single sign-on capability to access an enterprise system, real-time patient monitoring displays or even the mere electronic capturing and storage of patient data in an EHR system.

Product benefits, on the other hand, focus on the outcomes or results users will (hopefully) experience by using the product or service. A robust benefit description refers to a problem faced by consumers and provides an explanation as to why prospective customers become actual customers. To illustrate, a five-blade razor functions to remove as many whisker stubbles as possible, more than one can achieve using a razor with less than five blades. The benefit to the user of a five-blade razor versus a one-blade razor then is "smoother skin." In a similar fashion, a single sign-on enterprise system exists to overcome the inefficiencies and inconveniences of managing multiple logins and passwords when working within an enterprise system. The

HIT benefits of a single sign-on system might include enhanced user satisfaction with the enterprise system or improved user efficiency.

There may be a multiplicity of reasons why people use features over benefits when discussing the value of a product. One explanation involves "assumed intuitiveness." IT professionals like marketers spend a great deal of time "in the weeds" examining common problems experienced by their target audiences. Immersed as they are in addressing why a product's feature will make the ideal customer's life better, IT professionals and marketers occasionally assume consumers will automatically make the same logical connections between product features and product benefits as they have already made. The reality is product benefits may not be immediately obvious to some laypeople, and assuming the intuitiveness of the connection may be counterproductive to one's messaging efforts.

Another common misstep marketers and IT professionals make is equating the time and effort that went into developing a new feature, with its value to consumers. Product representatives tend to highly value product features that are "progressive" in the marketplace or reflect a significant investment by product developers. As harsh as it may sound though, consumers generally do not care how many late nights a vendor's engineering team stayed up to get a product to market. Their primary interests are to satisfy their personal needs and wants. The projection of valued personal interests onto end users, such as innovative features, may not necessarily support one's efforts to demonstrate the value of a HIT initiative.

Communication professionals need and use both features and benefits in persuading their intended audiences. This mixture of features and benefits is evident in the STEPS™ model. The domains of the STEPS™ Framework for example, arguably reflect both features of HIT (Treatment/Clinical; Electronic Secure Data; Patient Engagement/Population Management) and benefits of HIT (Satisfaction; Savings). Though the STEPS™ domains reflect both HIT features (e.g. electronic data) and benefits (e.g. savings), the intent of the framework is to focus on the beneficial evidence of HIT.

To help users of the STEPS™ Framework appropriately differentiate health IT features from health IT, users can employ a tool marketers frequently employ in their marketing communications efforts: the feature-benefit matrix. Formatted as a grid with one column for features and several more columns for benefits (Figure 8.1), the feature-benefit matrix helps marketers ensure their messaging is consistent and relevant.

To use this tool, IT leaders list the features of a HIT product in the far-left hand column and then use the adjacent columns ("Benefit A," "Benefit B"

Feature	Benefit A	Benefit B	Benefit C
1.			
2.			
3.			
4.			
5.			

Figure 8.1   The Feature-Benefit Matrix.

and "Benefit C" or as many as needed) to list the associated benefits. Using this format of feature-benefit matrix can help one quickly and easily identify each of the unique benefits offered by a HIT product. This, in turn, can help users map each benefit identified to the appropriate STEPS™ pillar.

One feature/multiple benefits. The feature-benefit matrix exercise helps underscore a significant aspect of the STEPS™ Framework that arguably adds to the complexity of the model; HIT features and benefits are not mutually exclusive ideas. It is very possible for a singular HIT feature to be associated with multiple HIT benefits. To illustrate, consider the feature-benefit matrix for enterprise computer systems with single sign-on capabilities (Figure 8.2). Though far from an exhaustive listing of benefits, the following demonstrates the multiplicity of health IT benefits that can be associated with a singular HIT feature.

Subjective classification. Another notable aspect of the feature-benefit matrix that adds to the complexity of the STEPS™ Framework surrounds the subjectivity in classifying HIT benefits. Leveraging the single sign-on example cited above, it is possible to categorize Benefit B (reducing the

Feature	Benefit A	Benefit B	Benefit C
Single Sign-On	Enhances overall clinician satisfaction with the enterprise system	Reduces the amount of time clinicians waste in accessing disparate information resources	Increase revenues by enhancing the productivity of clinicians.

Figure 8.2   HIT Features-Benefits Matrix Example.

amount of time clinicians waste in accessing patient information) under the Treatment/Clinical domain, as well as the Savings domain. Enhancing clinician efficiency in the treatment of patients is both a clinical workflow improvement (STEPS™ domain "Treatment/Clinical"), as well as a time saving (STEPS™ domain "Savings"). While it is possible to represent this one benefit under both pillars, the decision of how to display this benefit to varied stakeholders rests on the IT leader's preferences.

Direct and Indirect Causality

Another complexity of the STEPS™ Framework involves the causal linkage between HIT interventions and HIT outcomes. Recognizing the variances in causality will help users of the STEPS™ Framework in assessing the persuasiveness of the evidence in supporting the value of HIT.

The STEPS™ Framework functions to help IT professionals catalogue the various evidential manifestations of HIT benefits. It reflects an understanding that the use of HIT can have some type of positive impact on varied stakeholders, albeit patients, clinicians, organizations, etc. What the model does not account for though, is the degree to which a specific HIT intervention is associated with a positive outcome. Some HIT interventions clearly have a cause and effect linkage to specific outcomes. To illustrate, the reduction in the turnaround time to access physician notes in an EHR (an outcome) when a voice-recognition software program used to convert physician recordings of patient notes/summaries (HIT intervention) replaces transcriptionists (non-HIT intervention), reflects the direct causal benefit of using HIT. If the turnaround time was 120 minutes pre-implementation of the voice-recognition program, and the turnaround time is 20 minutes post-implementation, then the amount of time reduced by the HIT intervention equals (120–20) 100 minutes. This outcome clearly links to the HIT intervention.

Other outcomes are less directly connected to HIT interventions. Physician satisfaction with HIT for example assumes physicians are assessing some aspect(s) of the technology's performance (e.g. ease of use; ability to create efficiencies, etc.) and not a mere reflection of the technology in and of itself. That a voice-recognition system, for example, can reduce the turnaround time to access physician summaries in the EHR by 100 minutes, is what can by extension positively impact physician satisfaction. As such, evidential support for the value of HIT involving satisfaction in the STEPS™ Framework is always mediated by the performance of the technology. A similar relationship surrounds evidence involving the financial impact of HIT. Technology has to produce some tangible operational outcome before one can calculate the financial impact of the technology. To illustrate using the voice-recognition example again, if the voice-recognition program can reduce the turnaround time to access physician summaries by 100 minutes, and staff time equals $1 per minute, then the voice-recognition program can yield (100 × $1) $100 savings for each physician summary.

Given the variances in causality, a general rule of thumb of the STEPS™ Framework is that the "T", "E", and "P" domains reflect direct beneficial evidence of HIT interventions, whereas the "S" domains tend to reflect the indirect (or downstream) impact of HIT. As a result of these evidential differences, the "TEP" domains tend to be the most persuasiveness pieces of evidence in supporting the value of HIT.

Summary

The STEPS™ Framework is a useful approach for helping IT professionals catalogue the various evidential manifestations of HIT benefits. Yet there is a complexity to the categorization of evidence in the framework IT professionals should recognize when using the model. First, the distinction health IT "features" and HIT "benefits" can blur. Some people cite HIT features as evidential support for the value of HIT, when the more persuasive approach is to highlight HIT benefits. Second, while the STEPS™ model focuses on the causal linkages between HIT interventions and HIT outcomes, there are variances in the extent to which these linkages exist. As a rule, the "T", "E" and "P" pillars generally reflect direct beneficial evidence of HIT interventions and tend to reflect the most persuasiveness evidence supporting the value of HIT.

CASE FOR DISCUSSION: CHILDREN'S HOSPITAL BOSTON

Ranked among the first in more specialties than any other children's' hospital in the nation, Children's Hospital Boston has proactively worked since the 1990s to implement electronic medical records. Daniel Nigrin, MD, CIO, speaks about the strategies for implementation of an EHR at

Boston Children's, including the importance of integration of patient data, the future challenge of connecting on an external level and benefits derived from their system. The EHR system at the Children's Hospital provides technology that supports:

- Reduction in medication errors.
- Drug interaction dosage and allergy checks.
- Bedside medication barcoding.
- Legibility of notes and orders.
- Filmless radiology.
- Accessibility of records, labs and tests.
- Patient portal – patients have access to their own records.
- Analytics and decision support.

With these tools, measurable improvements have been achieved. These include:

Clinical improvement:
- Serious medical errors reduced by 50%.
- Decreased medication and fluid errors by 25% through bar coding

Efficiency improvement:
- Verbal medication orders reduced and sustained at 1.2%, down from 3.1% in 2007.
- Space savings: area containing 9,648 linear feet of unused rolling storage shelving will be incorporated into a department renovation.

Financial performance:
- Reduction of medical waste by 30% resulted in approximately $1.6 million savings per year.
- Back-end speech recognition savings/cost avoidance: FY09—$269K.

Source: HIMSS Analytics, 2010: Children's Hospital Boston.

DISCUSSION QUESTION

In the above case, how are the "financial savings" measures related to the improvement measures in "clinical improvement" and "efficiency"?

Reference

HIMSS Analytics. Children's Hospital Boston. 2010. http://www.himssanalyticsasia.org/emram/stage7caseStudyCHB.asp. Accessed August 9, 2018.

Appendix A

The appendices that follow offer integrative cases that reflect values in the HIMSS Value STEPS™ Framework. The student will find it useful to seek out those values and consider how they were achieved and the challenges faced by the organizational leadership, clinical staff and others involved in implementation of the health IT and/or as users of it.

These case studies tell the story of the journey of healthcare systems to achieve Stage 7 on the HIMSS Analytics EMRAM.

INTEGRATIVE CASE #A.1: TEXAS HEALTH RESOURCES

PROFILE

Texas Health Hurst-Euless-Bedford

- Established 1973
- Member of Texas Health Resources since 1997
- Licensed beds: 304
- Active medical staff members: 354
- 1,589 employees
- 12 board of trustees members—community members and physicians

THE CHALLENGE

As part of the THR strategic plan for our Hospital Operations Innovation initiatives, the nursing departments across the system were standardized to a benchmark within the National Database for Nursing Quality Initiatives (NDNQI). The challenge was in determining the staffing needs for patients based on their actual care needs or "Acuity." In the past, the budgeted nurse staffing was based on history of volume, unit type and financial benchmarks. THR partnered with Clair Via to utilize an acuity-measuring tool that is determined by specific flow sheet row documentation in our EPIC Care Connect Electronic Healthcare Record.

IMPLEMENTATION OVERVIEW

Key participants involved in the process: Clair Via has been used as our scheduling system and has interfaced with payroll for the nursing departments for a period of years. In 2015, the THR System Acuity Implementation Committee was created to integrate the Clair Via acuity measurement system with our Electronic Healthcare record nursing documentation to facilitate system-wide implementation and long-term support. Each wholly owned hospital facility has a clinical representative that serves on one of four sub-committees: Implementation, Reporting, Support and Policies and Procedures. Acuity driven Target Staffing is the amount of patient care, by skill and time of day, required to assist each patient to progress toward an improved clinical state, based on each patient's acuity level plus the workload associated with admission, discharge and transfer events (Cerner, 2018). The first entity went live with acuity-based staffing in 2015 with a pilot phase. Texas Health HEB went live on June 12, 2016. Preliminary preparations included acuity audits by trained super users to test the evaluation of care needs, accuracy of documentation and acuity levels. Charge nurses and managers were trained with face-to-face class times as well as system-wide webinars. Census (including admissions, discharges and transfers) is updated in real-time with integration between Invision, Care Connect and Clair Via. Charge Nurses see updates in the acuity system based on patient care needs at every four-hour intervals during each shift and are able to make staffing decisions based on this information. Staff can be better utilized and resources managed through this system.

RESULTING VALUE/ROI

Tangible and intangible results achieved. Tangible results include savings (cost, time, resources), reduced medical errors, outcomes (i.e. patient quality and safety, financial or operational) and creative use of physical space formerly occupied by hard on-site files. Intangible results include such things as clinician and patient satisfaction, etc. Cost savings occur due to improved staff utilization and management, resource allocation based on true patient care needs and optimized staffing models across all entities. In 2017, nursing budgets will reflect both the NDNQI benchmarks and our acuity data. Making this data available real-time to the nursing units helps us identify a true increase in patient acuity, direct caregivers needed and re-allocate our resources. For our quality metrics, we are now evaluating our unplanned transfers and mortality for subtle acuity changes along with our alert systems for sepsis, shock index and vital sign changes in our Electronic Health care system.

LESSONS LEARNED

Moving from a Staffing Grid model (based on HPPD metrics) to an acuity-based staffing model takes time and focus. This is a culture change from ratio-based staffing assignments to a much safer evidence-based method of making patient assignments based on the acuity needs of each patient. Assignments can be readjusted and balanced every four hours as well as patient's acuity score evaluated as an indicator of possible transfer to a higher or lower level of care. Readiness for discharge can be assessed as well.

Source: HIMSS Analytics, 2017: Texas health stage 7 case study.

Reference

HIMSS Analytics. Texas health stage 7 case study. 2017. www.himssanalytics.org/case-study/texas-health-stage-7-case-study.

Appendix B

PROFILE

The MetroHealth System consists of one acute care hospital and 17 ambulatory sites with nearly 500 attending physicians, close to 400 physicians in training, 1,200 nurses and 6,500 total employees. On an annual basis, The MetroHealth System records about 1,000,000 ambulatory visits, more than 100,000 emergency department visits (Level 1 Trauma Center), and approximately 28,000 inpatient admissions. The MetroHealth System is a teaching affiliate of Case Western Reserve University School of Medicine and is the essential (public) healthcare system in northeast Ohio.

EMR ADOPTION MODEL(SM)

Achieving EMRAM Stage 7 status facilitated real-time/near real-time scanning and elimination of paper processes to achieve a "paperless" healthcare system, enhanced bar-code medication administration and closed loop pharmacy medication preparation, among other quality, efficiency and patient safety initiatives. As an academic healthcare system, we also saw achieving HIMSS Analytics EMR Adoption Model(sm) Stage 7 recognition as a critical foundation for additional teaching and research opportunities.

IMPLEMENTATION OVERVIEW

A multidisciplinary team of administrative, operational, clinical and technical staff began planning for our EHR implementation in the mid-1990s. Between 1999 and 2002, we installed our outpatient scheduling, registration, billing and clinical care (documentation and ordering) modules in all of our ambulatory sites, and in 2004, we installed the emergency department module. In 2009, we installed the inpatient pharmacy system and converted to Epic in all of our inpatient clinical care areas. In 2011, we turned on the health information exchange, personal health record and e-prescribing, and in 2013 we implemented bar-code medication administration. In 2014, we transitioned to Epic in our operating rooms and for anesthesiology and laboratory information system.

As noted by David Kaelber, MD, PhD, MPH, CMIO, and Vice-President of Health Informatics and Patient Engagement: "Because we were an early adopter of EHRs in 1999, our 15-years to full HIMSS Stage 7 implementation has closely followed Epic's development of new electronic health record modules" (HIMSS Analytics, 2016).

RESULTING VALUE/ROI AMBULATORY AREAS

1. Depression screening
   We implemented the 9-question Patient Health Questionnaire (standardized depression screening tool) in all primary care sites to screen for depression and, with it, increased depression screening by 15-fold and diagnoses of depression by 23% (Palcisco et al., 2013).
2. Immunizations
   Immunization decision support was implemented for all pediatric immunizations as well as developed an automated messaging system to notify parents/guardians of adolescents due for immunizations, resulting in a 25% increase in adolescent immunizations (Hanson et al., 2007).
3. Pediatric hypertension
   Used EHR data to extrapolate isolated findings of under-diagnosed pediatric hypertension to expose system-wide under-diagnosis of hypertension in children and adolescents (designed as one of the top ten breakthroughs in stroke and cardiovascular medicine by the American Heart Association in 2007) Implemented clinical decision support to increase the diagnosis of pediatric hypertension by 50% (Bar-Shain et al., 2013).
4. Referral completion
   Developed Epic electronic health record-based processes to increase the 30-day referral completion rate from 48% to 63% throughout The MetroHealth System on all referrals. Resulted in

– 6,700 additional visits and
– $1 million in increased net revenue per month throughout The MetroHealth System

5. Hospital acinetobacter outbreak support
   By using a suite of electronic health record-based tools in support of an Acinetobacter (pathogenic bacteria) outbreak, the incidence of Acinetobacter in hospitalized patients was decreased by more than 60%.

6. Code status reconciliation
   The code status reconciliation in our EHR is used at discharge. This tool led to a 50% increase in the use of Do Not Resuscitate—Comfort Care and a 100% increase in the use of Do Not Resuscitate—Comfort Care Arrest—Do Not Intubate status in the transition from the inpatient to the outpatient setting.

7. Duplicate labs
   Implemented several duplicate lab clinical decision support tools that resulted in a 50% decrease in duplicate lab testing and saving of thousands of dollars in expenses annually (Noto et al., 2011).

8. Heparin errors
   After a sentinel event related to a heparin overdose, implemented a suite of electronic health record-based tools and redesigned a number of EHR processes related to heparin. In the three years since implementing these tools and changes, no heparin errors with patient harm have been identified.

9. System-wide health information exchange
   The MetroHealth System has conducted health information exchange more than 250,000 times and currently exchanges information thousands of times per day with other systems that have the same EHR, i.e. the Veteran's Administration, and the Social Security Administration.

   We have shown that when robust health information exchange occurs, about 80% of the time a test is not ordered that otherwise would have been ordered, and approximately 15% of the time, an inpatient admission does not occur that otherwise would have occurred (Kaelber et al., 2013).

Our EHR has also generally helped to:

1. Increase research grant funding.
2. Attract and retain trainees and attending physicians.

3. Decrease malpractice cases and led to more efficient resolution of malpractice cases.
4. Decrease operational costs and increase revenue in numerous way.

LESSONS LEARNED

Technical and "Non-Technical" Issues

EHRs are 10%–20% about "technical" details/issues and 80%–90% about "non-technical" details/issues, which are critical to getting the EHRs implemented and adopted.

Implementation and Post-Implementation

Although implementing EHRs is a huge undertaking, implementation is only the "tip of the iceberg." To achieve the full value of these systems, most of the work occurs after the system is live. The staffing, resources and structure is different during the implementation and post-implementation part of the cycle, but do not overlook post-implementation. Once a system is implemented, the post-implementation phase is ongoing.

Informatics

Developing an informatics team—made up of clinical staff who understand the technical functioning of the clinical information systems—is one of the keys to successful implementation, adoption and ongoing use of a clinical information system, and seems to be frequently overlooked/undervalued.

References

Bar-Shain D, Palcisco K, Greco PJ and Kaelber DC. Using advanced electronic clinical decision support to improve the quality and recognition of abnormal blood pressure values in children. 2013. Pediatric Academic Societies Meeting. Washington DC. [Oral presentation.]

Hanson ML, Gunn PW and Kaelber DC. Underdiagnosis of hypertension in children and adolescents. *Journal of the American Medical Association* 2007 Aug 22; 298(8):874–879. PMIS:17712071.

HIMSS Analytics. Metro health stage 7 case study. 2016. https://www.himssanalytics. org/sites/himssanalytics/files/The%20MetroHealth%20System.pdf. Accessed August 3, 2018.

Kaelber DC, Waheed R, Einstadter D, Love TE and Cebul RD. Use and perceived value of health information exchange – one public healthcare system's experience. *Am J Manag Care* [special health information technology issue]. 2013; 19(10 Spec No. 10):SP337–343. PMID:24511888.

Noto A, Greco P and Kaelber DC. An analysis of clinical decision support for repetitive urine culturing. 2011. American Medical Informatics Association Annual Symposium. Washington DC. [Poster.]

Palcisco K, Kaelber DC, Cebul R and Stokes L. Using electronic health record (EHR) tools to improve the screening and recognition of depression. 2013. American Medical Informatics Association Annual Symposium. Washington, DC. [Abstract presentation.]

Appendix C: HIMSS Value STEPS™ Framework Domains

HIMSS Value STEPS™ Framework Domains, Sub-Domains, Examples		
STEPS™ Value Domain	Sub-Domains	Value Examples
Satisfaction	Patient satisfaction	Increase in overall patient satisfaction/survey score
		Increased use of patient portal
	Provider satisfaction	Improved communication with other providers
		Improved communication with patients
		Improved quality of life
	Staff satisfaction	Improved internal communication
		Increased staff morale/job satisfaction
Treatment/Clinical	Safety	Reduction in medical errors
		Improved use of clinical alerts
	Quality of care	Improved continuity and coordination of care

(Continued)

		Improved management of diabetes
		Improved management of CHF patients
		Improved clinical documentation
		Reduction in hospital acquired infections
		Reduced admissions and readmissions
	Efficiencies	Decreased redundancy in diagnostic testing
		Improved access to health records
		Increased use of e-prescribing tests/drugs
Electronic Secure Information/Data	Evidence-based medicine	Availability of genetic data for clinical decisions
		Improved analytics reporting
		Increased access to data for clinical research
		Increased access to evidence-based clinical guidelines
	Data sharing	Improved security of data and patient records
		Increased clinical trends tracking
		Increased information sharing among providers
	Data reporting	Improved quality measures reporting
		Increased number of patients tracked

(Continued)

	Enhanced communication	Improved communication between providers/staff
		Improved communication with patients
Patient Engagement/ Population Management	Patient education and engagement	Improved distribution of patient educational materials
		Improved patient engagement
		Improved patient access to their medical record
	Prevention	Decreased obesity
		Improvement in smoking cessation
		Increased immunizations
		Increased screenings
Savings	Financial/business	Increased patient volume
		Increased patient revenue
		Reduction in days in accounts receivable
	Efficiency savings	Improved workflow
		More efficient use of staff resources
		Reduction in transcription costs
	Operational savings	Improved inventory control
		Improved use of space

Index

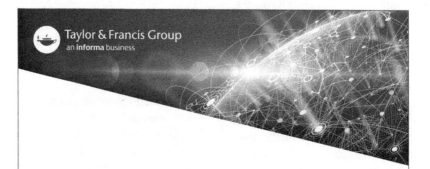